Taking Control Through Minimalism, Decluttering and a Minimalist Budget

2-in-1 Book

Discover how to Embrace Minimalism, Detach from the Unnecessary, Avoid Consumerism and Control Your Finances

Finding Ease Through Minimalism and Decluttering

Learn How to Detach Yourself from Unnecessary Objects and Thoughts and Get Your Life Back in Control

© Copyright 2019 - All rights reserved.

The following book is reproduced below with the goal of providing information that is as accurate and reliable as possible. Regardless, purchasing this book can be seen as consent to the fact that both the publisher and the author of this book are in no way experts on the topics discussed within and that any recommendations or suggestions that are made herein are for entertainment purposes only. Professionals should be consulted as needed prior to undertaking any of the action endorsed herein.

This declaration is deemed fair and valid by both the American Bar Association and the Committee of Publishers Association and is legally binding throughout the United States.

Furthermore, the transmission, duplication, or reproduction of any of the following work including specific information will be considered an illegal act irrespective of if it is done electronically or in print. This extends to creating a secondary or tertiary copy of the work or a recorded copy and is only allowed with the express written consent from the Publisher. All additional rights reserved.

The information in the following pages is broadly considered a truthful and accurate account of facts and as such, any inattention, use, or misuse of the information in question by the reader will render any resulting actions solely under their purview. There are no scenarios in which the publisher or the original author of this work can be in any fashion deemed liable for any hardship or damages that may befall them after undertaking information described herein.

Additionally, the information in the following pages is intended only for informational purposes and should thus be thought of as universal. As befitting its nature, it is presented without assurance regarding its prolonged validity or interim quality. Trademarks that are mentioned are done without written consent and can in no way be considered an endorsement from the trademark holder.

Table of Contents

INTRODUCTION 7

CHAPTER ONE - UNDERSTANDING MINIMALISM 10

What is Minimalism? 10

Minimalism vs. the Culture of Consumerism 11

8 Life-Altering Benefits of Minimalism 12

The Relationship between Minimalism and Decluttering 14

The Warning Signs Signaling Clutter that You Cannot Ignore 15

CHAPTER TWO - LAYING THE FOUNDATION FOR YOUR BEST MINIMALIST SELF 19

Powerful Principles to Help You See the World as a True Minimalist 19

Everyday Minimalist Habits to Get You In the Zone 27

CHAPTER THREE - DECLUTTER YOUR HOME 101 35

Light Decluttering: How do I start? 35

Tips to Maintain a Permanently Decluttered Home 36

Questions You Must Ask Yourself Before You Buy Anything 47

The 30-Day Wishlist Strategy 48

CHAPTER FOUR - FREE YOURSELF FROM EMOTIONAL AND MENTAL CLUTTER 49

Factors that Facilitate Mental Clutter 50

Must-Know Practices to Help You Deal with Mental Clutter 51

How to Identify Your Core Values 58

Everything You Need to Know About Decluttering Your Relationships 59

CHAPTER FIVE – THE SECRETS OF FINANCIAL MINIMALISM 69

How Minimalism Can Help You Financially 69

Minimalist Tips to Help You Achieve Financial Freedom 71

CHAPTER SIX - ADVANCED HOME DECLUTTERING 75

A Room-by-Room Decluttering Guide 75

Tips for Getting Rid of Sentimental Clutter 78

The Best Way to Decorate and Design a Minimalist Home 79

CHAPTER SEVEN - DIGITAL DECLUTTERING 81

The Principles of Digital Minimalism 82

Important Advice for Defeating Digital Clutter 83

CHAPTER EIGHT - PERFECTING THE MINIMALISM EXPERIENCE 86

Why We Need Experiences More Than Material Things 86

Experiences that are Better Than Any Material Object You Can Buy 88

The Experiences that Make Far Better Gifts than 'Stuff' 91

Conclusion 95

Minimalism & Decluttering

INTRODUCTION

It can happen in the blink of an eye: one day you wake up and discover your life is clogged. You realize you don't really need most of the stuff you currently own. You discover you have slipped into the black hole of clutter and if care is not taken, you could slip even deeper and lose the true essence of your life. The possessions around your home could fall into any of these categories: things bought, things Inherited, and gifts received. At one point or another in your life, all these things served a particular purpose. You were happy with them, until you realized you no longer needed them. These items were tossed into a space of your home and began to occupy it permanently. Over time, stuff has accumulated and now you've lost control. It's like you are a protagonist in a horror movie and all these items have invaded your home with the sole aim of tormenting you.

You have picked up the right book. I can assure you of that. In these chapters, I will be exposing less-known ways of reclaiming your life, your mind, and your finances. It is one thing to notice the presence of clutter in your life, but it is another thing to know how to get rid of it. People tend to ignore the clutter in their lives, not because they are comfortable with it, but because they don't know how to relieve themselves of it. This can be the most frustrating of all. In fact, it is better not to discover the presence of clutter than to discover it and not know what to do about it. Truth is, clutter can easily become so large and towering that you can't help but notice it. These monsters of clutter are why I embarked on this journey. With my wealth of knowledge in your arsenal, you'll defeat clutter in no time.

I like to refer to myself as a "Declutter Agent." It may sound strange (you may be wondering, "Is that really a thing? Do people study that at school?") but we exist, believe me. People in modern day are finally willing to let go of the junk hoarded in their basements and attics, and experts like me help them achieve this aim. From the young age of seven, I began what I fondly call "An Experiment on Clutter." It is a work in progress, but I have discovered valuable information on how to starve clutter of their life force and hinder their growth. There is an antidote to this monster's bite!

The antidote is this: minimalism and decluttering. The two go hand-in-hand and the wonders they work in your home and life are startlingly transformative.

In the ignorant mind, the word 'minimalism' can sometimes conjure visions of poverty, extreme frugality or even stinginess. This view is completely inaccurate. Minimalism puts you in control of your life. Know how they say, "less is more"? Minimalism and its approach to decluttering will help you reclaim all personal spaces that have been eaten up by junk. Your home will finally become a place where you can live freely, unobstructed, and life will become more enjoyable and fulfilling, overall. It is possible to achieve this!

The study of minimalism and decluttering is one that I have dedicated a great deal of my life and career to. And many of my past clients rave about the positive results they've seen after employing the methods taught in my seminars and webinars. Many of my clients have overcome depression and anxiety, and the majority have learned to regain control over their chaotic lives. These glowing testimonials have compelled me to compile an up-to-date and highly comprehensive archive of my methods. These are the same tools and techniques I teach to my clients. People who adhere to my instructions rarely find themselves coming face-to-face with clutter again. All you need is the right dose of self-discipline and you are good to go.

The approach I bring to the topic of decluttering and minimalism is a simple and straightforward one. I understand that some of my readers will be first-time students of the topic, so it'll be best if it is watered down for their easy understanding. The act of decluttering can be mistaken as a sequence of actions that involve the process organizing or putting things in their right places, but I tell you there is more to it than that. The ultimate success of the process is dependent on mindset and a determination to maintain consistency. I will not only teach you how to declutter your home, I will also show you how to declutter your life, your mind and your thoughts. It is an all round process, and if one facet is ignored, then success might never be attained.

Think of the clutter in your life as an ever increasing monster. There is no stopping its growth. As time goes on, you will acquire more household items, kitchen utensils, children toys and clothes. All these things will accumulate and pile into corners of the home. All of these might not appear dangerous in the real sense of danger, but clutter is a life poison, a virus that slows down the operating system of your life. Understand that your home, mind, business and family are all at stake because of the presence of clutter.

A Chinese proverb says that the best time to plant a tree is twenty years ago. The second best time is now. The solution isn't only in taking action, but in taking the necessary action NOW! No matter how stirred you may be by the points detailed in this book, you will never achieve tangible minimalism success until you begin to apply the methods listed. You'll feel a push while reading this book; don't hold back. Draw out a small timetable for yourself and stick to it. Make a conscious effort to declutter your life. Remember, only you can help you out.

CHAPTER ONE - UNDERSTANDING MINIMALISM

What is Minimalism?

The term 'minimalism' originated from an extreme form of abstract art that was first developed in the U.S in the early 1960s. This form of art depicted imagery that was stripped down to its barest so it could be more easily understood while passing across the intended message. The qualities of minimalist art were that they held a form of purified beauty for any beholder willing to look past their stripped down nature. In essence, the basic message that minimalist artists wanted to send was that there is always more in less. And as counter-intuitive as that sounded, the art form excelled and became popular with time. To help you understand its popularity, Alberto Giacometti's simple human-scale bronze sculpture of a pointing man sold for a whopping $141.3 million in May 2015.

The truth is that the concept of minimalism has been popular for centuries, even though many people have mistakenly assumed it to be a modern phenomenon. Minimalism has always been linked to pure, intentional art and design concepts. But it is also much more than that. Minimalism is about identifying the basics, the necessities, and sticking with them while eliminating all excess.

Our lives in this modern world are far from minimalist. Our society is constantly fed with the notion that the more you have, the more you are. Each day we are stuffed with more adverts and promos urging us to get this latest designer watch or those trendy new shoes. It's a cycle that never seems to end. A lot of us spend time chasing after these things, blinded and convinced they'll provide us with the happiness we need. I have been there and I can tell you that these shiny new objects do not give you the happiness they promise.

Here is my own simple definition of minimalism,

Minimalism is a form of intentional living that allows you to reassess your priorities and reconsider what truly brings value to your life. Minimalism strips you off distractions and allows you to reconnect with what brings you freedom.

As you read on, you may want to tweak this definition to better encapsulate your experience. Wants and needs vary from person to person. It's likely that minimalism achieves your needs in a different way.

Minimalism vs. the Culture of Consumerism

There's no way to sugarcoat it: we live in an obnoxiously consumerist culture. The pressure to consume is so strong that everywhere you look there's a new billboard shoving an attractive product in your face. Just walking outside can incite a battle of the mind and urges.

Being influenced by culture is normal, but some aspects of this culture can be quite damaging if care is not taken. Consumerism and minimalism are two opposing forces in modern day. The ultimate victor depends wholly on you. Every day, these large companies shell out millions of dollars in search of your attention. Social media influencers who act as their minions are also intent on getting you to consume more. The dominant message sent with these ads is, "You need to buy this product. Wealthy and attractive people all around the world use this product – and don't you want to be like them?"

Advertisements are crafted daily with this intended message in mind. But ask yourself, "Did I need this before I saw the advertisement? Or do I only need it now that I know it exists? Is this need real or is a company trying to make me feel this way?" These are the basics of minimalism. It starts with the mind. It starts with talking to and cautioning yourself. No one is saying you should not be influenced by YouTube or Facebook ads, but learn to probe the intention of the sellers. What do they really want from you? Will this product offer value to you or does a company just want your money?

8 Life-Altering Benefits of Minimalism

There are many obvious benefits of decluttering, such as having a more organized home, but the benefits of minimalism go much deeper than that. Here are some of the biggest benefits of minimalism:

1. Emotional Stability and Clarity of Mind

The connection between the mind and the number of possessions we own is a strong one. Research has shown that a few minutes a day to clear out the trash, make the bed and deal with the laundry can massively impact our mental state and provide peace of mind. When we're not surrounded by mess, we subconsciously relax. When there aren't a million tiny objects to distract us, we can think more clearly and make better decisions.

2. Reduced Stress

Knowing that once you walk into your home, you'll find a pile of clothes on the bedroom floor, plates in the sink and books littered on the dining table is enough to make a lot of people fear the doorknob. It can create a psychological drain and if you're not careful with it, depression may even set in. Clutter eats up space in your home and can create a sense of claustrophobia, a feeling that your own home is being taken over. You must deal with clutter before it chases you out of your own home.

3. More Room for Things of Value

As I've illustrated, less is more. When you purge your life and flush out the things that aren't important, you are creating more space for things of value. As long as your life is filled with junk, there will never be space for what you really need. I don't just mean in terms of physical space, but also financially. If you're spending all your income on new clothes, how are you ever going to afford a comfortable new sofa? Call me crazy but I think it's much better to own three pairs of quality socks than a hundred torn ones.

4. Better Relationships

Minimalist principles apply to all aspects of our lives, and that includes our personal relationships. When we practice minimalism on a deep level, we become a magnet for better friendships and relationships. You see, even certain people in our lives can be considered 'excess.' How many of your friendships truly bring value to your life? Who are you only friends with because you want to seem more popular? Minimalism teaches us that having few but close connections is better than having many impersonal acquaintances.

5. Improved Time Management

Clutter kills time. Have you ever searched for a bunch of keys in a disorganized desk? No one wants to go through that on a busy morning. Clutter is a beast that can eat into your time. We waste a lot of time searching through needless junk for the items we really need. Think of how much time we'd save if we didn't have to endure this confusion!

6. A Happier Planet

The earth is at the mercy of your minimalism. Less clutter in our homes means less waste in landfills and in the oceans. A lot of our clutter cannot be recycled. If we continue to purchase clutter, companies will only continue to produce it. And let's face it, we don't need most of these shiny objects. If you live a minimalist life, you can go on with a clearer conscience. You can rest easier knowing you are not contributing to the world's growing trash pile.

7. Sense of Purpose

Motivation can return to your life after the process of decluttering. It is almost like you are starting life all over, like you have been reborn, giving yourself a second chance. Once you have gotten clutter out of the way, confusion leaves and a sense of clarity sets in. I have often heard people say that once they lose motivation or interest for a certain activity they stop for a while and clear their surroundings. There's nothing like the beauty that comes with the creation of space. It's a good way to remind yourself of the control you have over your life.

8. **Emotional Freedom**

Emotional freedom comes when we learn to let go of emotional clutter. We accumulate emotional clutter when we hold onto feelings such as malice, jealousy, grudges, and hatred. When you find the strength to settle scores, pay off debt and move on from mistakes, your mind is relieved. When we hold grudges or feel jealous of someone, this exhausts our emotional system. Imagine what you could have accomplished with that energy if you hadn't lost it to such negativity.

The Relationship between Minimalism and Decluttering

As I explained in my introduction, minimalism and decluttering are two capsules used together to cure the clutter disease. People use both words interchangeably thinking that they mean the same thing. This is an understandable mistake. Although they cover the same concepts, they are not the same. One serves as a springboard leading to the achievement of the other.

Decluttering is the beginning process for people who want to take back their lives and own their spaces. Some people who indulge in decluttering have no intention of living a minimalist life. For them it is just about decluttering today, waiting for the clutter to accumulate again, then decluttering again. For them decluttering is a form of therapy, a way to clean up their lives on a temporary note. As a whole, decluttering is hardly a life changing process. It is just like brushing your teeth every day or vacuuming the sitting room each morning. The result of decluttering is often never permanent. Most people often go back to decluttering every other month or year.

Minimalism and decluttering both share the same theme, which is the removal and disposal of excesses in one's life. Decluttering consists of a simple process while minimalism is an adopted lifestyle. Minimalism is a mindset where the practitioner has committed to only having things of value and importance in their lives. Minimalism helps to curb the excesses of consumerism so that decluttering will not be needed. It is all about living and surviving with less so that more intangible rewards can be attained.

The Warning Signs Signaling Clutter that You Cannot Ignore

Clutter is an ever-increasing monster, but the only problem with this monster is that you never notice its growth until the day it jumps out of the closet and grabs you by the neck. Just like a sickness, not everyone sees it coming. Study these signs and compare them with what's going on in your home right now.

1. **You're Overwhelmed in Your Own Personal Space and Private Life**

In my years of experience dealing with clutter, I can say that this is probably the most dangerous sign of all. It manifests itself in small ways. You wake up in the morning and remember all the appointments you have for the day and instantly begin to feel overwhelmed even before getting out of bed. Frustration sets in and the essence and joy of life is lost.

Once you get home, it seems like your own house has locked you out, even though you have the keys. You discover piles of confusing items that keep jeering their faces at you. You become confused and pray earnestly for the next morning so you can run away from the mess in your own home. Guess what? Clutter in the home is equal to clutter in the mind. Your home is yours and yours alone and you have to deal with it one way or another.

2. **A Distracted and Unfocused Mind**

All monsters are unattractive and they can easily cause distractions when they arrive. No one can remain calm in the presence of a gorilla-sized humanoid with horns and razor-sharp fangs. That is how it is with clutter as well; you can't get anything done in its presence because it causes one to feel scattered and unfocused. Even seemingly minor clutter like unwashed dishes can create anxiety and steal away focus. Clutter isn't only a hindrance to productivity, it can also get in the way of relaxation.

3. **Buying to Impress**

If you often feel tempted to buy particular items because you want to impress family and friends, even when you don't really like these products and may not need them, know that you are living a cluttered life. Chances are that most of the other things you own were bought with this mindset and are creating clutter in your home. Anytime you are forced to seek validation from an outside source other than yourself, the happiness you find will be shallow and never fulfilling.

4. **You Have Trouble Finding Things**

Clutter swallows things up. When this happens, you'll have to beg this monster to release your things back to you. Have you ever wondered why you can't find the T.V remote, or your socks, or even a screwdriver when you actually need it? The answer is simple: clutter. These things have lost their rightful places in your home.

Books under the bed, spoons in the living room, knitting needles stuffed between the cushions: if any of this brings your home to mind, then you need to declutter. If you find yourself constantly misplacing things, then it's possible you own too much stuff. Once all extraneous items are cleared away, it immediately becomes easier to find items in the home.

5. **You Own a Junk Drawer**

Junk drawers are gradually becoming common in today's world, and this is a result of people having far too much stuff. The junk drawer is a dumping ground for miscellaneous items. Frankly, you do not need a junk drawer. If you can't find a home for certain possessions, then you should honestly rethink their necessity. As its name suggests, most of the objects placed in this drawer are junk.

6. **You're Ashamed of Your space**

Does the thought of a friend coming over to visit you send shivers down your spine? Do you start frantically cleaning and tidying when someone calls to say they are coming over for a brief visit? If you answered 'yes' to these questions, you likely have a big clutter problem. Let's get to work on it right away before clutter becomes the landlord and you become the tenant.

Minimalism & Decluttering

CHAPTER TWO - LAYING THE FOUNDATION FOR YOUR BEST MINIMALIST SELF

Powerful Principles to Help You See the World as a True Minimalist

To reap the full benefit of minimalism, you must be willing to pay the price mentally, psychologically and physically. As we've established in the previous chapter, minimalism doesn't just deal with the physical aspect of your life; minimalism goes deeper, penetrating one's mindset and attitude towards life. These following principles will help you prepare yourself for the journey ahead of you.

1. Your Possessions Don't Define You

Contrary to what most people believe, you are not what you own. Your possessions do not define your worth and value. Unfortunately, many people make purchases with this misconception in mind. If you want to look good, go ahead, and if you want the latest accessories, go for it, but don't make these purchases with desperation. And do so without accumulating clutter.

It is not easy to practice minimalism in the world we live in today. We are constantly reminded of how we could and should be wealthier. We are bombarded by messages telling us the more we have, the more attractive, worthy, and interesting we are. But how many times have the products we've bought delivered on these promises? At the end of the day, we still have the same insecurities and the same obstacles. Chances are, even when you bought what you thought would be a quick-fix to something, you continued to encounter that problem. Your possessions will not fix what you're unhappy with. How much you own does not determine your worth.

Minimalism & Decluttering

This may be a sign that you don't feel fulfilled in your life; once you chase what truly makes you happy, and allow yourself to be defined by your accomplishments, you will no longer need material objects.

2. See your possessions for what they truly are

It is time to take a bold step and honestly assess all your possessions. Look around your home and observe what's creating clutter. Ask yourself why you spent so much time and energy acquiring, maintaining and storing all these objects. The stuff we own can be divided into any of the following categories: functional objects, beautifying items, and sentimental things.

Functional objects get certain jobs done. They are needed to help us carry out everyday activities. Some of these are essential for our survival while others exist simply to make our lives better. It is important you understand that not everything you want is necessary for your survival. You might like to believe that, but it isn't the truth. Any functional objects that make day-to-day living easier are welcome in your new minimalist world. A home can function just fine in the absence of a skateboard but cannot do the same in the absence of cooking pots. Both things add value to a home, but the value of one outshines the other.

Beautifying items are brought into the home because they add aesthetic value to their surroundings. Art should be appreciated and embraced since this can sometimes add ambiance or a sense of calm to a room. But be careful as too many beautifying items can still form clutter, especially color clutter. Observe your shelf for a while and notice the presence of mismatched antiques. Just because you appreciated that sculpted object a few months after your mother's death does not mean that it should have a lifelong space in your home. We outgrow things and our love for them, and that is completely normal.

Things that do not fall into any of the previously mentioned categories usually turn out to have sentimental value. These can consist of gifts, inherited belongings, or objects that remind you of a particular point in your life. Sentimental objects remind you of the places you have been, the people you met along the way and the experiences you had.

When assessing your belongings, answer these questions:

- What value does this add to my home?
- Would I consider replacing this if it ever gets broken or lost, or would I be relieved it was finally out my hands?
- Did I need this item before I acquired it?

3. **The joy of simple living**

When you simplify your life, you are left with the basic, most necessary things that give you value and joy. Limit your purchases and acquisitions to the bare minimum so that you allow only what you need into your life. Having only the essentials in your home is a major component of minimalism. Doing so helps to prevent the influx of domestic waste (which is a form of clutter in itself). Strive to reduce your consumption rate so that you only have the things you need to satisfy your immediate needs.

Most consumers in our modern world can't even take comprehensive stock of the things they own because they own so much. Simple living helps you to stay aware of and responsible for your possessions. Perhaps you asked yourself one morning, "Where is my navy-blue polo shirt?" And even after weeks of searching you were unable to locate it. That is one major sign of clutter. You own things that you do not need or use and this has given birth to irresponsibility.

4. **Crave the availability of space**

Every once in a while, we just want to have a breath of fresh air. Have you ever tried doing that in a room full of other people? Of course not, because it brings no comfort. In fact, the room full of people is likely why you need that breath of fresh air. You'll find yourself breathing in cologne and body odor. It would be different if that space was clear. Naturally, we all feel calmer in an empty, clear space.

The absence of space causes distress. When there isn't enough of it, claustrophobia begins to eat you up. Many people believe their space problem can only be solved by moving to a larger house or compound. Within a few months of arrival, however, the clutter begins to form again on this new environment. Don't run away from your lack of space; tackle it head on and start creating more space. This is what minimalism helps you achieve. Every space becomes enough for you because you have mastered the art of creating more whenever you need it.

As I established in my introduction, clutter is a monster that eats up space. One day you wake up and discover that all the space you once enjoyed has disappeared and you wonder what happened. It was a gradual process and because space is silent, it uttered no word as it was being swallowed. Don't fret over your lost space. You might have lost it as fast as a finger snap but it is not lost forever. All you have to do is get rid of needless belongings.

You must take into consideration the amount of space you have in your home before buying more stuff. Remember that the space in your home is not emptiness. It brings its own aesthetic value. It allows all who live in that space to breathe easier and freer. Learn to crave this feeling, instead of stuff.

5. Less stuff means less stress

People rarely consider this, but it takes a lot of physical and mental energy to manage all the stuff you own. After purchasing the item and that fleeting moment of what I call the 'buyer's high,' the fun of the situation begins to go steadily downhill. Not only does this item now take up space in your home, but you must expend energy keeping it in place and out of the way. And should the item break, it'll cost more money and time to have it repaired. Soon, it begins to feel like the products control your life, instead of the other way around.

The stress attached to accumulating possessions comes in stages. A sense of alienation and deprivation sets in once you discover that you don't own a particular item. "Gosh! I'm so out of style!" you might find yourself thinking. This is when stress begins to develop. There's a sense of feeling irrelevant if you don't own the right product. Then there is the stress related to acquiring the item. You start window shopping, surfing the web, and scrolling aimlessly through Amazon. Soon, you have an increased heart rate.

You realize you can't quite afford the item, but you put it out of your mind and buy it anyway. Your excitement outweighs your rational mind, but the stress seeps in once you click that 'confirm purchase' button. When the item arrives, you're filled with that familiar euphoria, but this doesn't last long. Once it loses its shine, it ends up in the same corner with all the other things you once loved, but that no longer interest you. It becomes another thing to throw out of the way when you can't find what you need.

Take a moment to remember life before you owned so many possessions. Everything was a whole lot simpler. You possessed that unadulterated joy of a minimalist, and probably more money, too.

I'm not trying to convince you to live in the woods, feeding on slugs and earthworms, with only a bed of hay and a wooden spoon. I'm only asking you to reflect. Imagine yourself without half of the possessions you currently own. Consider your life without your entire mug selection or the books you've owned for years but have never read. Consider your life if you only owned the handbags and purses you *actually* use. Chances are, your life is not any worse. And think of all the stress you'd be removing from your life!

6. **Contentment is powerful**

I can't stress this point enough: contentment is the foundation upon which a minimalist lifestyle is built. A greedy person or hoarder will never be able to practice minimalism to the fullest, unless they undergo a complete transformation. What's crazy about the modern world is that most of us *are* content with the things we already own – until we're harassed by the idea that something better exists and told we need to buy it now.

Once your basic needs as a human being are taken care of, then happiness should be in place. Your happiness should not be dependent on the things you own; when that happens, happiness becomes unattainable. When you learn to appreciate the little you have, you begin to see abundance in everything and life becomes even more enjoyable. Focus on what you have instead of what you don't have, because once you begin to compare your life with the lives of people around you, your hunger for more stuff never rests. Stuff cannot fill the void of your deep discontentment and dissatisfaction.

You must practice the art of believing that you have enough before you actually have enough. 'Enough' is, after all, a thing of the mind in the modern age when most of us have our basic needs satisfied very easily. It all has to do with self-control and self-discipline.

7. **Protect the flow of things into your life**

How easy is it for useless things to get into your life and settle there? Everyday more consumables pop up in search of a new home, and unless you practice self-awareness, your home is at risk of inviting this new clutter in. Protecting the flow of things into your life means you should only allow things of value in – the things that provide you with undiluted joy, free from the need to please or make others approve of you.

These clutter-building objects do not have legs or wings. We must ask ourselves, "How do they find their way into our homes?" Either we buy them or they are gifted to us.

Your home is your personal space; it is the only part of the whole world where you can be king or queen. A conscious effort must be made to protect the home from these unwanted materials. Before anything finds its way into your home, assess your entire situation.

The necessary questions here include:

- What role do I see this object playing, if any, in a few months' time?
- Is there a place in my life for this item right now?
- What is motivating me to purchase this?
- How long has it been since I purchased something that functions the same way?

You may be wondering, "But what do I do about gifts, giveaways, or freebies?" Politely refusing an item sometimes works fine, but most people don't have the mind to do that because of their relationship with the giver. If you truly feel you need to collect that item, go ahead, but make a mental note to take that item out of its place in a few months, and have it discarded, donated or sold. Don't allow this clutter to settle down in your home. Your home is not a dumpster.

8. Live life free from the shackles of Possessions

The best minimalists are those who have learned to manage the effects that possessions have on their well-being. The idea here is to loosen the grip that your belongings have on your identity. The emotional strongholds that we build around these objects can be binding and if we aren't careful, they may lead to suffering. Detaching from your belongings means finding emotional freedom, looking beyond the monetary value of possessions to see the real value of life.

The benefits of practicing detachment from possessions are numerous and life-altering. This will eventually lead to a less greedy personality. When you are no longer plagued by an insatiable hunger for stuff, you will find far more life satisfaction. You can finally find freedom from the material hang-ups of the modern world. Have you ever heard of families ruined by conflict over who gets to inherit a recently deceased loved-one's stuff? That doesn't have to be you!

Minimalism is a wakeup call to stop feeling defined by your belongings and to form attachments with aspects of life that create deeper joy. Help out in the community. There are new experiences beckoning to you. There are numerous people you can meet and forge new relationships with.

Although we might want to shy away from the topic of death, it will befall us all at some point. When your time comes, all the useless items you've become attached to will be left behind and serve no purpose. The things you leave behind will be what you're remembered for. While preparing for your minimalist life, take a few moments to sort through your belongings and consider what impression this will leave. This is not to make you fear or worry about death, but to make you understand that only a few things in your life are actually worth the space they occupy.

9. You don't have to own it to enjoy it

Consider this question: why do you have to own it to enjoy it? Adding a new object to your pile of clutter is not the only way you get to experience the benefits of that object. In this day and age, we are so eager to own things (and sometimes, even people) which we can call ours and *only* ours – but this is a silly way of living life. Items that are communal in some way are just as good. By borrowing or renting an item, you can still make good use of it without ever having to worry about its long-term place in your home. If you need a new book, why not borrow one from a friend or the library? If you need an outfit for a fancy event, there are many companies offering rentals of high-end clothing for short-term use. Rentals are much cheaper than purchases. Not only is this kinder to your wallet, it's also kinder to your home.

Everyday Minimalist Habits to Get You In the Zone

You probably knew this already, but minimalism isn't just a habit, it's also a lifestyle. For die-hard minimalists, it can even seem like a religion. For a little humor, consider clutter as the evil of this minimalist 'religion.' Just as every other religion has its everyday rituals to help followers stay connected to its teachings, minimalism also has its own routines and habits that serve a similar purpose.

There are simple habits that should be implemented daily or weekly into your new minimalist schedule. These habits may seem small but they'll create a world of difference. Most of these daily rituals can be carried out in mere seconds, without eating up too much of your time. Before we get into the habits of minimalism, let me explain a great strategy for integrating healthy new habits into your life.

- **A life hack for developing better habits**

When we try to create better habits, we tend to make things hard on ourselves. It doesn't have to be this way. Want to know a secret? You should find a way to attach the habits you want to develop to already existing habits. If listening to podcasts is part of your daily schedule, try doing this *while* doing something you don't enjoy as much. You could attach this habit to the less-enjoyable act of washing the dishes. Or you could connect the habit of getting ready for bed with the practice of clearing your desk space. When it comes to creating new habits, this is a tried-and-true way of making them stick.

MINIMALIST HABITS

1. Fire up your minimalist mindset every day

Start each day by reading or watching anything that has to do with minimalism. This way, you can ensure you always stay motivated. Refreshing your mindset about the powerful benefits of minimalism will help to keep you on track, especially on days you feel like giving up. Do it first thing in the morning because that is when your subconscious is most active and receptive to information.

Almost every ad on social media or TV is a promotion of consumerism. The more you pay attention to them the more you find yourself drifting away from minimalist teachings. Be diligent as you adopt this new lifestyle. Make a conscious effort to fill your morning, and in essence, your day with information that matters and information that will benefit you. Subscribe to minimalism channels on YouTube and follow minimalism influencers on Instagram. Start every day by revving your minimalist engine.

2. Find your tribe

The people you spend time with will inevitably influence your actions. You can't nurture a minimalist dream while hanging out with materialistic people. One party will influence the other, and I'll tell you now, materialism is far more catching than minimalism. No matter how disciplined you are as a minimalist, it will take a great deal of emotional and mental energy to not get sucked back into a world of consumerism.

If the people in your life live in alignment with minimalist teachings, it will be easier to make this new lifestyle stick for good. Minimalism will no longer be something you have to *try* to embody; it will simply be the new norm. You will not think otherwise. This is why it's important to find your tribe. This doesn't mean you can't socialize or get to know any other people (obviously!), it just means you need to be aware of who you surround yourself with and how that will impact your new life changes. Evaluate your life now and consider which people will be good and which ones will be bad for your promising new chapter. Come up with methods that will protect you from their materialistic ways if you ever need to hang out with each other.

3. Gratitude

Gratitude is powerful. Gratitude energizes the smile on your face and makes you the most attractive person in the room. This habit is easy to incorporate into your day, but as I've said, you will need a drastic change of mindset. The only difference between a grateful and ungrateful person is their mindset. Once you start looking at the world through the lens of gratitude, you instantly feel far happier.

Every morning, just before your kids or partner are awake, take out your special notebook or journal and list out three things you are grateful for. This can be anything! Your kid scored 80% on a pop quiz after you helped them study? Show gratitude for being blessed with a smart child. Is it a cold, wet, and miserable time of year? Show gratitude for having shelter from such terrible weather. Just think, you could be out there in the freezing cold right now! Contentment is only a thought away when you make gratitude a daily habit.

4. Fill your life with experiences, not stuff

Value the experiences and memories that life brings your way. People will not remember you for the things you brought home from the mall, but for the experiences that you gave them while you were with them. Go somewhere fun. Go see a waterfall and experience the beauty. Cook someone a fantastic dinner. Shared memories and experiences are the rock on which friendships and relationships are built. People will always remember you for how you made them feel.

5. Learn to say "no" when necessary

Never underestimate the power of saying 'no.' Despite how small the word is, it carries a lot of weight and power. Lives have been changed and saved just because someone dared to say 'no.' As a minimalist, you have to cultivate the habit of saying no whenever it needs to be said. Saying no doesn't make you a mean person. In fact, it's saying yes when you shouldn't or when you don't mean it that makes you a coward. Do you find yourself unable to say no to people? Do these people always end up coming back? It's probably because they know they'll never be refused by you. Look around, some of the most respected members of society are those that say no at the right time. They are not easily swayed into other people's schedules and plans.

The habit of saying no can be learned with constant practice and over time. Saying no to others is saying yes to yourself and releasing yourself from future engagements and commitments which may turn out to be clutter in your schedule. Or worse, your bank account.

Say no to the kids who might want extra toys. Say no to friends who might want you to host a party even if you don't have the time and resources to do so. Say no even to your own self, when you mind is begging you to buy a new novel at the bookstore when there are a hundred in your home library that you haven't even opened.

6. Plan a simple but nutritious meal

Simplifying your meals will teach your taste buds and overall palate to enjoy and accept the natural taste of food. The need to add extra flavoring to your meals will be reduced. This lifestyle change will prevent more packaging from finding its way into your home. A constant attempt to outdo yourself in the kitchen can be a drain on your time and energy. Have a meal plan that can be easily repeated with variety from time to time. Your shopping process will turn out to be much more streamlined and clutter will be far more controlled.

7. Employ space control mechanisms

Creating more space in your home is a decent way to deal with clutter, but it's not the best way. What you may have only succeeded in doing is providing more space for the growth of clutter. Instead of looking for how to create space in your home, employ mechanisms that will help you control the space that you already own. People have been building increasingly large homes and yet clutter still exists. Once we see the availability of space, it is our human nature to want to fill it up with stuff. For minimalism to take full effect, we must learn to suppress this urge.

Have two boxes placed at strategic points in your home. These boxes are for possessions that you are making up your mind to let go of. One of them will contain the things you want to sell or donate and the other will contain things that you want to discard. With that settled, stay alert and aware of what's eating up space in your home. Identify the things that have lost their value in your home and choose to either donate or discard them. This simple trick works wonders and clears up space within months of continuous practice.

8. Minimize your debt

Debt is a form of clutter on its own. It weighs you down both emotionally, financially and in your relationships with people. It may not work in exactly the same way as material clutter, but debt accumulated over time will always come with frustration, anger and depression. Minimalist philosophies stress the importance of preventing the creation of debt, but in the event that it has already happened, you must make plans to pay it all off and remove the burden.

Don't fret. It might seem like an insurmountable giant, but a step by step approach will nail it in the head. First, make up your mind to not accumulate more debt. Before you call your friends to ask for a loan or worse, buy something expensive on your credit card, consider deeply if it is necessary. Most times we fall into debt just because we're so convinced we'll get our act together later. If you can't do it now, why will later be any better?

Do some calculations and figure out what your weekly or monthly income is. From that sum you can set out a certain percentage for paying off debt, bit by bit. If you can make the payments automatic or a direct reduction from your paycheck, do it. It will also help to develop emergency funds; in other words, money you can fall back on when the time arises. Set up an account and send small chunks of your earnings into this account. Save money in this account over time and resist all urges to spend from it, unless you absolutely have no other choice and desperately need the money. No, your 'wants' do not count!

9. Go for quality every single time

They say anything worth doing at all is worth doing well. I say, "Anything worth buying at all is worth buying in high quality." Substandard goods always turn out to be cheap because the sellers are sure that they won't last long in your possession. When we catch sight of these low prices, however, we find it hard to resist making the purchase. Inevitably, wear and tear occurs and you return to buy a new set of these same substandard products. Over time a growing pile of low-quality products appears in your home, when you could have just bought one high-quality product instead. Not only is this a waste of space, in the long run it's also a waste of money. Don't be fooled by that cheap price tag! Quality comes with the extra cost and your peace of mind is worth that extra cost.

Minimalism & Decluttering

CHAPTER THREE - DECLUTTER YOUR HOME 101

Now it's time to get into the minimalist decluttering process in real detail. We have successfully established the foundations of minimalism, the importance of minimalism, and the habits that will set you on the right track towards a life of unrestricted freedom from material objects. This chapter will walk you through essential decluttering processes. Like everything we've demonstrated so far, it's vital that you make these practices part of your routine, and not just a one-time activity.

Light Decluttering: How do I start?

One of the most significant drawbacks of starting any new habit or task is figuring out where on earth to begin. When decluttering the home, there is always a place to start. When you look around your home and see clutter lying around your living room or your bedroom floor, something speaks to you and says: "You can't do this. It is too much. Where will you put all of this stuff?" Don't get worked up and overwhelmed by fear. All you need to do is adopt consistency. Decluttering doesn't happen in an instant. It is a process that takes time because it also took some time to build up. As you take time to practice it more and more, you begin to get better and better at it. Soon you find yourself naturally engaging in the process. It has become part of you.

The key to decluttering from scratch is to take everything out of its designated place. Turn the drawers upside down and pour out all its contents. Strip down the closet to bare hooks, rods, and shelving. Don't forget that you will need a free space to dump out the things to be either discarded or donated. I suggest you start with one small area at a time so that the room you are presently working on does not become crowded with materials and hinder free movement.

Pretend that you're starting life in your home all over again. Seeing belongings in a different place will change your perspective about its arrangement. And pouring out your stuff can help you identify some items that haven't been in their proper place for a while. Don't hesitate to take anything out of its designated space. Pick a portion of the house you are most comfortable with and start. There are many places you can begin decluttering, and no single one is better than the other. It can be your bedroom, or the attic or the basement. Just pick a spot. When you are there, you can look for a smaller portion of it and work on that: under the bed space, the wardrobe or the shoe rack. Don't neglect any part of it because every overlooked corner holds clutter that can grow if you don't pay attention.

Tips to Maintain a Permanently Decluttered Home

1. **What stays and what goes:** Once you have poured out clutter from its hiding place, you need to start the sorting process. This is the point at which you must find the root cause of all your clutter. The sorting process has three categories: Keep, Discard, and Donate. You will need three containers for each of these. Boxes will also work well to help you out, mostly, if you need to deal with smaller items. If you have a smaller box, you can use it for things that you have presently not made up your mind about. As you sort through, you will come across items that have you pausing and feeling confused about whether to throw them or keep them. Throw them into the box and go back to them later so they don't slow down your progress.

The possibility of you finishing up with boxes full of undecided materials is very high. You don't have to fret. Seal it up and place a date on it with a marker. Give the items some time and come back to sort through them again. By this time, you will have a clearer mind and judgment about the future of these belongings in your life. You should not get too entangled in the decision of having a box full of undecided items. That is a form of clutter on its own. Don't just dump it in the basement and forget it because you feel that you do not have the emotional stamina to let go of those things. The point here isn't to find a different storage place for these items, but to keep the decluttering process as fast and smooth as possible.

☐ **The discard box:** The content of this box can be called the 'Discardables.' Don't linger on the name, as these items are basically trash. These items serve no purpose in your life. Don't get carried away and do not drop any of them into the 'Keep' box. The truth should always prevail in your decision-making. There are things you might feel still have value but inside of your heart you know they are trash; you just don't want to let them go because they hold certain memories or ideas about what you want to be. The discard box is filled with things that are hard to let go of. If it cannot be fixed, then you should let go of it.

Recycling some of these items is an option. Have your immediate environment in mind as you sort through these items. Go on YouTube and search for information about stuff that can easily be recycled for a greater purpose and value. Proper disposal of trash should be an important consideration as you sort through the pile. Where will these things end up? What can be repurposed and reused?

☐ **The Keep Box:** This will contain all the things that you want to keep. The possessions here will include everything that still brings value to your household and life, things you truly cherish, and things that are still functional and useful. If you haven't used some items in years then you should know that they don't belong in that box. They will be more useful in a donation box or in the box of undecided items.

☐ **The donation box:** This box will contain items which are still useful but no longer serve any purpose for you. Examples are the expensive toys lying around the basement, despite your youngest child already being in high school. You can give them out to new parents. They will have more value in their home than it will have in yours. Don't feel bad about letting them go. You are giving yourself freedom, and you are providing those items with a new life where they will be more appreciated. Something will keep speaking to you saying, "But you might still need this someday." Resist the urge to succumb to that thought. If you don't need it today, the possibility that you will need some other day is very slim.

Be more generous with the items in your donation pile. Rest assured knowing that someone out there will appreciate them. You might also be worried about where to take your donations. There are numerous religious organizations that are always in need of materials to give out to the less privileged. The Red Cross and other medical organizations accept your donations to deliver in relief of IDP camps around the world. All you need to do is carry out a little research on the internet, and the right people will come knocking at your door to help you take out your donations.

If you are reluctant to release your belongings to the world this way, then consider selling them instead. The cash will provide you with more value than the item lying around the house. Hold a garage or yard sale. You will be amazed by the amount of money you can make from one. There are a variety of things you can sell, from books to CDs, DVDs to golfing equipment. You will be shocked by how many people in your vicinity desperately need the stuff you have been hoarding.

2. A purpose for each item: It is very easy for the 'Keep' box to become flooded with items. Before any item should be taken back into your home and life, it is necessary that you reassess its true importance in your life. Ask yourself the essential question about each item you come across. Each item in your 'Keep' box should be making a noticeable positive contribution to your life. Everything else should not go in this box.

While you're going through these objects, you'll come across many things that serve exactly the same purpose. They may have different decoration or packaging, but they ultimately do the same thing. This is a case of duplication, and it should be appropriately handled and taken care of. Minimalism is about clearing excess from your life. Some of these items in the home can easily multiply and clog up drawers. Examples are pens, paper clips, or buttons. Save a reasonable quantity and do away with the rest of them.

Other items that aren't in the class of duplicated items should now be scrutinized. Probe the essence of each item, figuring out its value and how much that value is needed in your home.

The answers that come to your mind will guide you on where to place the items, either in a donation box or in a 'Keep' box. Some items might have some form of value, but the space they will provide once they are taken out of the way might be more valuable. Provide yourself with that new space and get that object out of the way.

While sorting through and making categorizations, you could consider having an objective and responsible friend who is also a minimalist around you. Their presence will provide you with enough drive to do the right thing. Having to explain why you want to keep one stupid item or the other can be embarrassing. You will look through your belongings with clearer eyes and understand why you need to let go of them.

While going through your stuff, keep in mind that you only make use of 30% or less of the things you own every month. And the difference is hardly ever noticed. Some of the things you hoard and protect so dearly will serve no purpose in your life throughout the year. But because there is space, you just decide to house them. Be more rigid during your sorting process. Look for the essentials that make up the less-than-30% and keep them. These are your most important possessions.

3. A home for everything: In your own home, each of your possessions should have their own homes - space they will occupy from now on. It should be at the core of your minimalist mindset: everything should have its place. It is an important principle of minimalism. It's much easier for you to keep stock and prevent stray items from moving into your home when there are designated places for everything. When this is in place, it is easier for you to identify things that should not be in your home and things that don't belong in your environment.

There are considerations to be made while making these designations, some of which include frequency of usage, size, fragility, and proximity. The house is already broken down into smaller units of rooms. Sometimes, if one is lucky or rich enough, the various rooms are broken down into smaller compartments or spaces to contain some special class of possessions or items. For example, cupboards in the kitchen can hold ceramics and cooking utensils, and walk-in-closets in the room can hold all clothes. An item's home should generally be closest to the place where it is most needed. If you have any clothes lying in a pile on your bathroom floor, it's time to move them to the place where they are needed.

The things you use most frequently are to be kept closest to you in a place where you can easily reach them. You will want to be able to access these items without unnecessarily scavenging and rummaging through your other stuff.

Once you have identified and designated a place for everything, it will help to label each of these places so that anyone coming into your home will know exactly where to put things after using them. Use it as a sort of address for each item. Even your kids will get used to it and follow this simple instruction. Get your family members actively involved in the decluttering process. If everyone has a mindset of decluttering and minimalism, it will be easier to tackle this monster. A collaborative effort does wonders. Clothes should be hung instead of piled on boxes or chairs. Take the utensils back to their hanging spaces instead of leaving them on the kitchen counter. Return books back to the shelf instead of leaving them on floors or chairs.

Once you come into a room, try to find items that aren't in their places and return them home. It will only take you a few minutes out of the hours of the day and the huge difference will be noticed in your household.

4. Keep clear surfaces - Wide and flat surfaces are major breeding grounds for clutter. Most items will end up on clear surfaces, there's no doubt about it. Take a look around your house. Surfaces like the dining table, kitchen counters or living room coffee table are likely loaded with clutter. This will build up gradually until the whole surface has been colonized by junk.

Clear surfaces add a certain kind of beauty to any environment that surrounds them. They offer endless possibilities. The clear surface in the kitchen will help you prepare a quick meal without any hindrance. A decluttered dining table will accommodate members of a family for breakfast. The importance of clear surfaces cannot be overemphasized. We don't realize the value of a clear surface until we find one covered in clutter. Suddenly, we can't put a single plate down, or we have nowhere to put our laptop down for work.

To ensure your surfaces stay clear, you must adopt a new attitude and observe some basic decluttering principles. Your surfaces should not be used as storage spaces. By all means necessary, your surfaces should be kept clean and clear at all times. These steps will help you:

Minimalism & Decluttering

i. Clear off every single object on that flat surface. Whether they should be on the surface or not is irrelevant at this early stage. They will be returned later, if they belong here.
ii. Once the surface is clear, stand back from it and notice the calm that comes with having a clear surface. See how inviting the surface is, observe the beauty of space.
iii. Identify what purpose that surface serves in your home. Is it a surface that serves a specific function (such as a kitchen counter) or is it used during moments of creativity? Maybe you want to use it for something totally different from its former purpose. Once you have successfully identified its function, you can now determine what will be going back on the surface and what shouldn't be on the surface.
iv. Try not to allow more than three objects on any table. Anything more than that will constitute as clutter. If it's an essential object, put it on a shelf or anywhere else closeby. Allow surfaces to remain as clear as possible until the habit sticks.
v. You can add up to two additional items for aesthetic value on these surfaces. These will serve to complement the surface and keep it from looking too bare or boring.

It is one thing to achieve a clear surface and it is another thing to keep it cleared. A lot of people clear up surfaces every day, but before the day is over they are back to square one. These tips will help you keep your surfaces cleared for a longer period of time.

- **Drop your items on the floor when you get home.** It is a basic instinct to drop things that come with you into a room on a clean and clear surface. It is relaxing to get the weight off your hands and onto a clear table or counter. Then they sit there for hours or days, neglected because they are not in your way. The most important rule is to get nothing on the surface in the first place, place those items on the floor and once they make you trip twice, you'll be eager to finally put them in their designated place. It might seem too extreme for you, but minimalism has to be extreme sometimes, especially if you are a person that easily gets comfortable with clutter. Discipline yourself against clutter. With time, you will notice an attitude shift that has you organizing anything you come home with at all times.

- **Wipe surfaces down at least twice every week.** Wiping surfaces down draws your attention to the clutter growing on them. As you wipe, put away whatever shouldn't be on the surface and move aside anything that gets in the way of your cleaning. Discard any trash or useless pieces of junk and return the surface back to its initial glory. Do this at least twice every week.

- **Leave nothing for later.** When you're in the process of clearing things away, it can be tempting to tell yourself you'll finish off certain tasks later. Don't do this. If you're done folding the clothes, send them over to the closet immediately. Don't leave them on the ironing table. You were reading a book at the dining table when you realized you had to pick the kids up from school. Send that book over to the shelf before you leave the house. This is a major key to leaving surfaces as clear as they should be. Adopt the habit of putting things away as soon as you are done with them. Once you get used to this, the house can almost clear itself.

- **Prevent the accumulation of small clutter.** We are all guilty of letting 'small clutter' build up in our homes. You notice it growing but you never quite recognize it as clutter until one eye-opening day. As the name suggests, small clutter consists of smaller items, such as pens, paperclips, or useless little knick-knacks. It takes a while for us to admit this is clutter because the objects are so small in size. It's only when they build into a pile or they continually get in our way that we begin to admit the obvious: it's clutter just like most of everything else.

- **Finally, don't ignore the largest surface in your home**: the floor. It's so large that we rarely notice if there's clutter on it. It can easily get nudged away to the side and we forget that clutter is there at all, especially since it's at our feet. Don't allow yourself to neglect the floor in your home. Soon your floor will be hidden under clutter and you will struggle just to go from the kitchen to the bathroom. This can kill enthusiasm and productivity. Reserve the ground for the rug, your feet and the furniture. Remove all other objects!

5. Use small units of organization - Your home will benefit from an organization system developed for the efficient arrangement of stuff. These small organizational units will consist of items that serve a related purpose. These items should be kept together in a specific storage location such as drawers, containers or boxes. This will make it easier to find them. If you are in need of a pair of scissors, you won't have to go searching through the toolbox in the garage; instead you can look through the small organization box containing sewing tools. When you are looking for the blue flash drive containing your son's graduation photos, you won't have to launch a search party to find it under the bed. It will be there lying in the drawer under the computer table. Doesn't that sound like the kind of life you want to live?

Organizing your belongings into smaller units with similar functions helps you keep stock of what you own, what you need and what you should release. It's only when you gather all the duct tape you own into one place that you realize there are three other rolls that you completely forgot about. This technique will help you curb the accumulation of materials that can grow into a clutter if left unchecked.

Once you've gathered all these supplies into their various groups, it's time to throw away the excess. Five hammers, sevens pairs of scissors, ten cutlery sets, and all these for a family of four. Do you really need all of these items in your home? Cut down the number of your possessions until you arrive at a more reasonable number. Reclaim your space from all of this excess. Go through these collections and save only the favorites.

6. Let in one and let another go - Decluttering can turn out to be a very frustrating process for people who haven't learned to control the inflow of stuff into their lives. You might have done everything perfectly, from categorizing your stuff and put them into their appropriate containers to keeping all your surfaces clear, but you may still find there is a lack of progress. There's still clutter in some parts of the house. You might wonder why that is. Think of your home as a hole and you hold a shovel, digging out sand from the hole. You dig as hard as you can and exclaim with joy once you see your hole is bigger than ever, with more space than you could have ever imagined. Now picture someone else shoveling in more sand just minutes after you've finished. Soon the hole gets filled up again. This is what seems to happen when some of us declutter. We end up almost exactly where we began. We clear away excess but then find ourselves *still* with excess. It doesn't matter how much sand you remove if you end up filling it with more sand later.

To prevent this from happening, do one simple thing: whenever you buy something new, get rid of something old. For every new book that finds its way into your personal library, your least favorite will leave the library. It is as simple as that. If a brand new ceramic bowl finds a space in the kitchen shelf, an older one should be given away.

7. Establish workable routines: At this point, due to the growing excitement that comes with picturing a decluttered home, you might think you have gotten all the principles at your fingertips. Yes, we have been able to thoroughly examine some of them, but it doesn't

Minimalism & Decluttering

stop there. Decluttering isn't a one-off activity where when we are done, we are done for life. Clutter is always waiting at your doorstep getting ready to invade again. You have to be on the constant lookout. It is just like a weed. You can cut it down as much as you want but until the root is addressed, it will always rear its ugly head again. The root of clutter is in your habits. What differentiates a minimalist from a non-minimalist are good habits. To succeed at minimalism, you must change the habits that govern your everyday life.

Vigilance is key. Live intentionally. Remember to always act as a gatekeeper and protect your home from excesses. Allow these principles to become second nature to you until you can no longer exist in the presence of the slightest clutter. Block unnecessary ads on your browser if you're materialistic and easily influenced by ads. Pay off debt and allow your mind to become more free. Cancel subscriptions that are no longer necessary for your business so your mail can stay organized.

Practice your decluttering process until you become nearly perfect. You may decide on a one-day-at-a-time approach. Dispose of one item each day. It won't take much effort or time. Just be consistent with it until you master it and it becomes part of you. One day you will discover that you have the drive to dispose of more than just one item. Once your donation or trash box is full, send it off to its specified destination.

Finally, set decluttering goals in your journal so that you know how much progress you are making. Tick off your goals as you achieve them as a form of self-encouragement and motivation. Don't forget to appreciate yourself for the efforts made once you hit a new milestone. Celebrate your resilience throughout the process and your mind will be fired up to do more. Just make sure you have fun with the process. See it as a game - a game that is capable of changing your life.

Questions You Must Ask Yourself Before You Buy Anything

A lot of people in this modern world are only trying to make more money so they can buy more stuff. And some others are even trying to pay off the debt they accumulated the last time they splurged. Don't get tangled up in this way of life. It is a cycle that never ends. To ensure you prevent this from happening, ask yourself the following questions whenever you feel the urge to buy something:

1. **Am I financially equipped for this purchase?**

This is where it begins. If you don't have the money for the purchase, why are you considering it in the first place? Consider the debt this might put on you. And consider what you're giving up by buying this product. If you buy this now, it means you can't buy something else down the road. Will this lead to you skipping a meal or having to live without a more essential product?

2. **Do I need this or am I just buying it because it's on sale?**

Impulse purchases are one of the biggest killers of minimalism and one of the biggest magnets for clutter. A genuine need will come up again and again. If it doesn't, then you can do without the item that satisfies that urge. Make sure that all your purchases are planned and not just a spur of the moment decision. Don't just buy it as soon as you want it; give yourself time to assess your situation and budget completely. If you're buying it for a valid reason and it's a necessary purchase, you will know.

3. **Do I already own something similar to this or can it easily be rented?**

Before you run off to buy something new, check to confirm that you don't already own something similar to it at home. You'll find some items in your home can be repurposed. Instead of going out to get some new containers, why not use the older ones that can just be washed and reused? If you are in need of a power tool to carry out a project, you can easily rent or borrow one from a neighbor instead of buying a whole new tool that will likely only be used once every half-year. By renting or reusing, you are saving yourself a whole lot of money.

4. **If I don't buy a higher quality product, what's the likelihood I'll have to replace this?**
'Quality over quantity' should be one of your mantras. The quality of the product should be your major priority because if you end up with something substandard, you'll have to shell out money for another one very soon. Why not save yourself the stress and buy something that will last a whole lot longer? Ask yourself: "Is the quality worth the price?" Maybe you want to get a new set of upholstery and you notice that the stitches are already coming undone on one side. Before spending all your money, consider using it to get something more long-lasting. It is pure joy seeing an item you bought years ago still serving its purpose with little to no wear and tear.

The 30-Day Wishlist Strategy

One way to tackle unnecessary purchases is by employing the 30 day wishlist strategy. The method here is simple: every time you feel the need to purchase something, write the name of that item on a list. This list can be anywhere: your phone, your journal, or even a note on the fridge. Each time you jot down an item, write down next to it what the date is. This will serve as a record of your spending urges and the day you felt each one. What you're going to do is wait at least 30 days before you consider buying this item. This will give you a lot of time to research the item and to see if you still want it after a lot of time has passed. For more expensive purchases, consider stretching 30 days to a longer period of time. If you decide you still want the item after 30 days or more, and you're sure you don't already own an item similar, then go ahead and buy it.

CHAPTER FOUR - FREE YOURSELF FROM EMOTIONAL AND MENTAL CLUTTER

We handled various ways in which we can take care of physical clutter, but clutter does not end there. Clutter occurs in our mind too. When people complain about emotional instability or depression, it is simply because of emotional clutter. They have ignored the main focus of existence and have begun chasing the meaningless things in life - things that only clog the mind and lead nowhere.

The building blocks of the mind are thoughts. Once our thoughts have been managed, then mind clutter can be dealt with. These thoughts can be positive, negative or neutral and just like your home is cluttered with possessions, your mind can also become cluttered with thoughts. If they are positive thoughts, then you are on the safe side. But that is not usually the case. Unfortunately it is not as easy to deal with mental and emotional clutter as it is to deal with physical clutter. You can't just discard a thought and expect it to not return. It doesn't work that way.

Sometimes it seems like these thoughts have mechanisms and minds of their own, and they can sometimes control you. Constructive thinking is necessary to help out with problem-solving, analyses, decision making, and planning, but despite all of this, the mind can produce negativity out of nowhere. This forms an inner distraction from the physical world around you. Have you ever come across someone on the subway that went past their designated stop just because they were deep in their thoughts? That signifies a dangerous emotional clutter. They are gradually losing touch with the physical world. These negative thoughts mostly spring up as a result of assuming that the harder you think about your predicaments, the easier it will be for you to get out them. Of course, we know perfectly well that it is a flawed ideology, yet we hold on to it. Why? It is because these thoughts have already created a stronghold in the mind. Soon you discover that you have been caught up in a constant loop of regretful thinking about your past and anxiety for the future.

These thoughts become such an integral part of your mind that you begin to think that there is nothing that can be done about it. You can't just shut down your brain and have it stop processing some thoughts. Negative thoughts are like a virus on a computer. You can reboot the system and it's still there when you turn it back on. You can sleep, wake up again, and your thoughts will continue to bother you. You have to deal with them squarely before you ruin your week.

All of your thoughts might be unconscious, but you can manage them by practicing intentionality. You have far more control over your mind than you think. You just have to be willing to exercise that control. Once you've managed your emotional clutter, you will discover an immense amount of creativity and inspiration that awaits you, hidden under all of that clutter.

Factors that Facilitate Mental Clutter

Before we set about trying to deal with mental and emotional clutter, it is necessary that we tackle the root problem. Where does all of this clutter emanate from?

- **Stress**

Stress can easily overwhelm you and overpower your motivation to live. Stress is associated with a variety of mental issues such as depression, anxiety and panic attacks. When combined with worries, negative thoughts and other concerns that burden our daily life, the problem only multiplies. Sleep becomes affected. Anger management issues may set in. Headaches and chest pains become the order of the day.

The stress can manifest itself in a variety of ways, for example, in a toxic work environment, domestic violence at home, or even a problematic child. Things turn out to be so complicated and intense that your mind loses the ability to control itself.

- **An Excess of Material Objects**

We handled this in a preceding chapter. Once your life and home become too clogged and cluttered with stuff, your mind begins to suffer. In the modern age, we are so eager to fill up our homes with useless possessions that have no true value and can be done without. All of this stuff contributes to time consumption, becomes a financial drain and induces anxiety.

People who are propelled to live their lives based on the quantity of physical possessions they own are always on the competitive side. Nothing is ever enough for them. They will always want to keep up with the latest trends no matter what it will cost them financially or emotionally. Decluttering your life of these things will ultimately help to curb the effects of negative thinking and anxiety.

- **A Litany of Choices**

Too much choice and variety can subtly lead to depression and anxiety. At first it might seem like the perfect life, to have a load of choices to decide from, but upon a closer analysis you will discover the unadmirable quality of it. What should be a decision that can be made in mere seconds will lead to days of agonizing contemplation. A litany of choices is brain-draining and stressful.

Must-Know Practices to Help You Deal with Mental Clutter

1. **Meditation**

Certain misconceptions may deter you from practicing meditation. Truth is, you don't have to be a Buddhist monk, a psychic, or even a certified witch to practice meditation. Don't get scared by the stories you hear about cave dwellers who meditate for months at a time. There are levels of meditation, and at this point, we are only going to tackle the basic levels of it. Meditation does not belong to people of a certain religious faith or spiritual inclination.

The only thing is that meditation and the reason for performing it vary from one meditator to another. For this chapter, meditation will be considered a tool to help you control your mind and your thoughts. You can practice meditation anywhere you feel like it. You don't necessarily need a quiet environment, but you must be able to achieve that quietness on the inside. That way, it will be easier for you to sort through your thoughts and pick out those that should be discarded. The benefits of practicing meditation are numerous, both for your physical wellbeing and also for the emotional side of your life.

The main point is to practice meditation consistently. You cannot reap its full benefits without constant practice. Commit to practicing meditation at a scheduled time every single day. That way, you will improve your ability to control your mind mechanisms and put them in check.

Meditation doesn't have to take long. All you have to do is to find a spot and sit still. Set out a specific time every day that you will carry out your meditation and stick to it. Don't choose an overly comfortable position so that you don't fall asleep while meditating. Turn off every digital device that's capable of producing noise or any distractions. Try and time yourself, so you know when you have done enough. For beginners, five minutes is enough time to meditate effectively.

Make sure you are ready for the process, and nothing else will distract you. For the next five minutes, focus on your breathing. Count the number of breaths you take in and out of your body. Notice how the air leaves you and returns into your nostrils. Observe the rise and fall of your chest region. Allow your breath to flow naturally; don't try to control them. This will help you build focus. At first, you might encounter problems keeping focus but try and return your attention to your breathing each time.

Close your eyes to avoid visual distractions. The goal of meditation is to shut thoughts out of your mind. By focusing on the breath, you are taking attention away from anything that causes you stress. Wave off the negative and store the positives so you can ruminate on them when the time finally arrives.

2. **Deal with the negative thoughts**

A lot of people go through life everyday with negative thoughts floating across the surface of their minds. They have become victims of a mental flood and if care is not taken, they may drown. The negative voices in their heads speak louder and louder until they can't even hear themselves. This form of negativity can be given strength and a stronghold in the mind if it is not challenged at the initial stage.

The first step is to notice these thoughts before they get out of control. Notice the pattern with which they operate in your mind. You can employ these strategies to help you out:

a. **Be Watchful**

You don't always need to have an emotional reaction to all your thoughts. Sometimes you should take yourself out of the scene and become a spectator. Observe what is going on in your mind. Notice how your thoughts interact with one another. Don't judge any of these thoughts negatively or positively. Just sit back and observe.

b. **See your thoughts for what they really are**

Although they are powerful enough to alter whole facets of your life, understand these are thoughts and nothing more. They are not real for the time being, but they have the capability to become real if you don't manage them.

c. **Put up a roadblock**

You own your mind, right? They you should be able to determine what comes in, what stays and what goes out. Whenever you catch yourself in a mental state that makes you uncomfortable, learn to scold yourself and stop the reaction. You can be vocal about your refusal to think those thoughts. Say, "I refuse to be caught by negative thoughts in this web of distractions." Build walls around your mind, strongholds that will serve to protect you whenever the time arrives.

d. **Know the causes**

Every negative thought in your mind is caused or triggered by a certain factor. It could be a person, another thought, a situation or even a physical state. The next time you find yourself wallowing in these thoughts, take the time to find out what triggered the thoughts. Chances are that they will be lying there waiting to be discovered and dealt with.

Write down the major triggers that come to your mind. Brood over them for a while and see if you can find any solutions to them. If it's something that you can solve by yourself, such as the reconciliation of a wrecked relationship or working on your own flaws, then go ahead and deal with these thoughts. If you discover that you have no power over the situation at hand such as an inability to travel because of bad weather or a miscarriage, make up your mind to be happy regardless. You caused none of it so there is no need to feel bad about it.

f. Occupy your mind

Each day you wake, you wake up with a clear mind, a tabula rasa. If you leave it empty, the mind has a way of creating something to do for its own self. Ever noticed how your mind is never empty, how at every point in time you are always ruminating and considering an issue? The mind is only inactive when you are asleep, and that is if it doesn't get overwhelmed by dreams. So once you wake up, give your mind something creative to do. Focus your brainpower on important projects that will help fulfill a long term goal. Give yourself something positive to worry about, like how you can get a PhD. If you find yourself stuck in traffic, pick up a book, and read or search for an insightful TED talk and listen to it.

3. **Subdue your mind under your control**

You are the boss here. Your mind belongs to you, and you should never give up control. Never let it run through the thoughts you don't want to process. Get your mind under control so that each time, you are pleased by the outcome it produces. You can achieve this by practicing the following:

a. **Identifying the wrong thoughts and replacing them**: The wrong thoughts are easy to identify; they can be spotted from miles away. Once your mind begins to process them, you notice a certain kind of weight hovering over you. And they are mostly exaggerated. Funny enough, the wrong thoughts are very pleasing to hold. You just lost your job at 50, and you begin to think, "I am a total failure. Can anything good come out of me?" You know you should not be thinking that way, but it seems very comfortable to dwell in that state of mind. Why? Well, no one thinks positive thoughts after a bad experience. If you examine that thought closely and truthfully, you will discover that it is not entirely true. Somebody somewhere admires you for who you are irrespective of your current financial state.

Instead of keeping yourself in that state, why not challenge your negative thoughts with positive ones? Reassure yourself that you are not a failure or a loser. Thinking you are one will not automatically make you a success. How many times have you gone into a job interview and one of the interviewers says, "Well, it seems you have always thought of yourself as a failure. We are going to give you the job to help you stop seeing yourself that way." It doesn't happen. In fact, people who breed negative thoughts are always repulsive to others. For every person who has given a negative comment about you or your work, there are about ten more making positive remarks. So why are you allowing that one comment to spoil your mood and corrupt your other thoughts?

b. **Accept the situation but don't get comfortable with it**

What do you do when the negative thoughts swirling around your mind are true? How will you be able to cope with the situation triggering these negative thoughts? It is hard to challenge negative thoughts with positivity when the truth is staring right at you. You just lost your home and all of your property to fire. Your grades are going down the drain and at this rate you are probably not going to graduate.

These are negative thoughts about situations that cannot be eliminated, but you can reduce the effect that they have on your mind by accepting the situation at hand, not the thoughts. It happened, and there is nothing you can do about the past, but you can change the future. Don't begin to nurture guilt about your carelessness, or go on about how things could have been better. You are only making your head foggier and clogging up your emotions. At this point, your best bet for a solution is to find peace of mind.

Accepting the situation will help you identify ways to improve or solve the problem at hand. There is always a brighter side, no matter how dim it may be, and it can only be identified with a clear mind.

c. **Take necessary actions**
Worrying and strategizing are two different things. Worrying is easier but its results can be bad for you. Strategy requires mental energy that most of us are not willing to sacrifice. The truth is that worry gets you nowhere; it is better you employ strategy. The downside of worry is that you expend so much energy producing negative thoughts and you never come up with a solution. All that energy you spent worrying could have been put towards strategizing, and perhaps your problem would be fixed by now.

Identify Your Core Values

A major challenge that people of this age face is the inability to identify what is truly important to their existence. In our world today, there are so many distractions that take away from what we need. We are bombarded by marketing and meaningless messages, and we rarely go inward, connecting to our inner voice. These things can become such an overload that the process of prioritizing our values becomes a major task. This makes it very necessary to reevaluate what is most important to us with each passing day. Rise over all of the societal noise by defining your core values.

Identifying your core values is one sure way to help you combat clutter, both physically and mentally. These principles will help you spend time, energy, and money doing the things that help you in the long run. The presence of core values enables you to keep focus. It is easier to spot distractions. A lot of the highest achievers of our age are people who have identified their core values. Once, during an interview, Steve Jobs stated that he kept his wardrobe streamlined to simple black turtlenecks, blue jeans, and New Balance sneakers.

Why? So that his wardrobe decisions didn't take up a lot of brainpower and he could focus on what really matters. That reply reflects the mindset of someone who has identified his core values. Try to picture how organized and minimalistic his closet probably looked.

How to Identify Your Core Values

Core values are not selected; they are discovered or revealed. It is easy to say that physical fitness is one of your core values, but when was the last time you actually exercised?

Deciding on your core values can be a daunting task, but what you find out about yourself will help you. In case you are unfamiliar with the core values terrain, let's go through some lists and identify some values that appeal to you. From there, you can streamline them into your perfect options. These can help you identify your core values:

a.   Your peak experiences
What do you consider a very important moment in your life? What makes that moment standout for you? What happened to you in that very moment? What values came into play to make this moment a very important one?

b.   Suppressed values
This is the opposite of the first one. Here, consider the values that cruised through you when you were the most angry and irritated. What got you angry during those moments? Those are your suppressed values. They never seem to rear their heads but they are there as relevant as ever.

c.   Brainstorming
Brainstorming involves more of a general search. You ask yourself questions that only you can answer. Pick a pen and a jotter and provide answers to these questions:
- What values in others attracts me the most?
- What drives me the most in life?

- What do I admire most about myself?
- What's one virtue I never want to lose?

While answering these questions, you will certainly run into moments of clarity and understanding and you will find your core values waiting on the other side of reflection.

d.   Ask the people around you

Sometimes people around you notice things you might ignore about yourself. For example, someone who is neat or organized might not necessarily understand how neat or organized he or she is until people point it out and commend them for it. It is just like using a particular cologne brand for years. Soon the fragrance blends in naturally with your nose and your olfactory nerves fail to interpret the smell because they have been doing so for a long time. Until the day someone points it out to you, you might never understand how much it has become a part of you.

Your core values are like this. People see your values before you even notice them, so their opinions can be very necessary for helping you identify these values. Look for the smart and observant people around you and ask them to define you and what they think you stand for. You will be amazed by the responses you receive. There is no way that you won't be able to identify your core values after following these steps.

Everything You Need to Know About Decluttering Your Relationships

You need people in your life, but they can sometimes be great hindrances. Once your relationships begin to falter, an unbalance sets in and soon, you're overcome by distress. The painful question, "Who can I trust?" begins to haunt you.

A popular saying goes, "We disagree to agree." Misunderstandings and reconciliations are some of the blocks that build and strengthen a relationship. But when these interactions constantly leave you worn out and emotionally drained, then it's high time you either try to mend broken bridges or remove the other party from your life.

You will never understand the importance of having healthy relationships until you try to imagine a life without any form of anxiety relating to the people in it. The most productive people are those who have created a perfect balance in every relationship, be it their relationship with their spouse, children, bosses or even the person beside them on the train.

Relationship clutter can build up in a variety of ways such as minor-major arguments, malice keeping, hatred, envy, jealousy, and the likes. Once they gain enough ground, they clog up your mind. Think back to the last time you felt annoyed by your best friend, or when you envied someone so much that you could taste the gall in your own throat. Think back and consider how heavy your heart felt in those moments. Then try to remember the feeling you had when there was an embrace of reconciliation. Can you feel how light your heart was in that moment and the deep breaths you took afterward? That's the beauty of a decluttered mind. Space is instantly created for something else, something worthwhile.

It is not just about having relationships but having quality relationships. Here's another saying: "It is better to make one true friend in a thousand years than to make one thousand fake acquaintances in one year." The beauty of relationships is not in quantity but in quality. The ingredients that make up a great friendship will include:

- Shared Interests
- Mutual respect and trust
- Understanding and acceptance
- Openness and honesty

- Healthy conflict resolution

Creating relationships is necessary to your existence and this is why it is essential to take your time choosing the relationships you should invest in. The primary reason why the loss of a relationship hurts so much is because of our emotional investment.

To begin with, work on your relationships. Start with yourself. They say, "If you want to change the world, start with yourself." If you want to change your relationships, you should start with yourself. It might be so obvious and glaring that the other person in the relationship needs to make a change too, but ignore that fact and start with your own change. It will help you heal and do away with all the clutter. After all, you can't change others except if they agree to change themselves or be changed. These strategies will help you build healthier relationships:

1. INVEST YOURSELF (YOUR TIME AND PRESENCE)

Once I saw someone post a picture of a friend and caption it, "Thank you for being there. Happy Birthday." It was the first time I had seen such a short message used on a birthday post, but it was very profound. That word 'there' meant so much to the person who had posted the picture. But what exactly did he or she mean by 'there'?

'There' signifies presence and time. That friend was available when he was most needed. Those kinds of friends are hard to ignore or forget. They make themselves available during the darkest times of our lives. They are present when it matters. How present are you in your relationships? How much of yourself have you invested? Here is how to invest yourself into a relationship:

1. Pay Attention

How do you feel when someone isn't paying any attention to something important you are saying? How does it feel when you know they aren't listening to something that means a lot to you? It is disheartening at best, and the chances that you will ever want to share a conversation with them are very slim. The truth, as bitter as it may sound, is that you have probably done it too, intentionally or unintentionally.

This mostly happens because of the numerous distractions in the mind that tend to monopolize your attention. This causes you to focus more on the crowd in your mind than on the person talking to you. Still, that is no excuse. Paying attention is the willingness to step out of all those distractions and listen, not just hear. Absorb the speaker and their words so that he or she will feel safe and comfortable talking to you. Make it all about the other person and what they are saying. Make each gesture count and try not to look distracted. These tips will help:

- Allow the speaker to dominate the conversation until they ask for your opinion
- Avoid unnecessary interruptions, except if you have something really important to say.
- Hear the full story before jumping to conclusions.
- Keep your gestures and facial expressions as neutral as possible.

Paying attention might look one-sided, like the speaker is the only one who benefits during the interaction, but learning to listen and shut out the noise in your mind is a huge benefit to you. In fact, it is one way of helping you declutter your mind and be more present.

    a. Positive speaking and encouragement

Language matters in every conversation. Don't rush to spill the contents of your mind. First, probe them and anticipate a reaction before you release them. Negative comments are products of negative thoughts and can be damaging to a relationship.

Pay close attention to the things you say during a conversation. It might not seem to matter, but the other person may feel differently. Recognize that each word is powerful and can create a different effect to what was intended. Don't say, "But you should have known better, especially with all of your education." Say, "It was a learning moment for you, and I am happy you learned the lesson." Don't say, "You acted so stupidly." Say, "I don't think that was the right thing to do at that moment." Speak with love and compassion.

Mastering the art of compassionate communication will make others want to talk and relate to you. Resist the temptation to be judgmental about other people's actions. Put yourself in their shoes and try to understand why they act the way they do. When you master the art of being kind in all forms, the people around you will mirror the same actions, and your relationships will blossom further. Of course, you already have an idea of how good that will be for your emotions. You will find peace in your inner world, and it will reflect into the world around you.

    b. Find reasons to love

No matter how bad a person is, there is always one reason to love them. Find that reason and cling to it. Of course, we have been told to love people unconditionally, but human nature makes that hard to do. Sometimes it is best to find reasons to love them even when it seems like they should not be loved. Reducing the negative thoughts you have about people in your life can significantly improve your relationship with them.

Studies have shown that when we think positively about others, it leads to increased contentment in life, kindness towards others in

Minimalism & Decluttering

general, hope and enthusiasm to build better relationships. How you decide to practice the art of positive thinking is up to you. You can do it by meditating on their good characters, or you can do it by saying positive things about them. The point of this practice is to transform your mind and declutter your emotions.

c. Eliminate comparison

Comparison is a prison that many people are locked in. Comparing yourself to others is one sure way to hold you back from any form of progress. Comparisons are fertile ground for breeding negative thoughts. "Am I good enough?" "Do I have what it takes to be admired like he or she is?" "Will I ever be that attractive?"

These thoughts can build up and get out of control until low self-esteem takes control of your thoughts. Most times, constant comparison can also lead to mild hatred for the person you are comparing yourself to. There is a high possibility of you viewing them as the reason for your unhappiness, even when this is an entirely unfair accusation. And there is no way you can have a healthy relationship with someone whom you feel this way about. Each time you see them, something shifts inside of you. Your mind begins to act abnormally.

You are on your own journey in life, and only you can understand your struggles. This is why we handled the issue of core values. A person who has discovered his or her true core values cannot be affected by comparisons to others because they already have a focus. Other people's journeys don't affect them.

Don't get me wrong, from time to time comparisons can take a positive turn, and that is something you should be on the lookout for. Use comparisons to motivate yourself and work harder to become a better person. Comparisons can help you identify places in your life that need to be worked on and improved. But when you begin to notice its excesses, and it takes a negative turn, turn it down a little. The mental effort involved in comparisons can drain you. Never allow it to grow out of your control. These tips can help you combat comparison:

- Accept Yourself

You are perfect the way you are, not because you are actually perfect but because you choose to believe that you are perfect. You can't change anything about yourself unless you have hundreds of dollars stashed up somewhere to spend on plastic surgery. Good luck with that and I only pray that you don't come out looking more messed up than before.

Instead of battling to change who you are, you can do a quick job of accepting yourself. No amount of comparison or worry will change who you are. Most people are more receptive to people who have accepted themselves for who they are. Self-acceptance is self-liberation and self-empowerment.

- Improve what needs to be improved

Change the things about yourself that can be changed. Are you insecure about your appearance? Work on your wardrobe or your hairstyle. Have you noticed that more people are attracted to someone who smiles? Then try to have more gentle facial expressions. Sometimes, no matter how much you try, you might never be able to match up to the people you admire and compare yourself to. Don't sweat it. Simply find something that makes you exceptional and work on it. Your core values and life priorities should be the main factor in helping you define your life. Sometimes we are attracted to qualities in others that we don't need. She has longer legs. So what, are you trying to become a long jumper? You are a writer, so the longer legs shouldn't matter to you. Focus on your strengths, the things that make you unique. Somebody out there that you don't even know yet thinks you are awesome because of them.

- Practice Gratitude

I talked about this in chapter three, but it still remains an important tip. You can forget to feel gratitude when you become too focused on what another person has. You begin to ignore the beautiful things that life has brought your way, simply because you are missing out on some other little things.

Gratitude is about committing to the bright side. It's a commitment to creating joy even when it feels like there's none at all. There are good things in your life and they should never be ignored. Focus on them for at least three to five minutes every day before going to bed or after waking up. I advise making gratitude part of your morning routine since it's a great way to start your day, but if you have busy mornings, a nightly gratitude routine works just fine as well. Take a moment to think about how blessed you are. It can be surprisingly liberating.

2. **RELEASE YOURSELF FROM YOUR PAST**

Carrying the burdens of the past is one way to hold yourself back from seeing the light in your relationships and life, in general. You may have been in some toxic relationships before now, but there is a time to let these lingering feelings go. It is natural for the mind to keep replaying scenarios and hurt over and over. However, this process should not take over any part of our lives. Having these memories return over and over can create wells of anger, guilt, and shame. These thoughts keep you stuck to the past, drain the positivity in the present, and rob your future. You not only clutter your emotions; you also imprison your mind and hinder its productivity.

It is hard to let go of pain from the past, but it can still be done. A lot of people have succeeded in doing it. You can, too. The benefits of letting go are enormous. Not only will you have more positivity because you create positivity, but you will likely also see more positive things come into your life. Why? Because we are a magnet for our life circumstances. Exude positivity, and you'll attract positivity. So, step one, let go of your past. Try the following tips:

a. Make Resolutions and Stick to Them

People get a strange amount of comfort from wallowing in pain, but we should always resist this urge. It gets nothing solved. Sometimes the people you feel have hurt you have no idea that they ever did that. Take action and find ways to resolve any issue that you feel needs to be resolved. Take out time to communicate with the person and clear the air. No matter how fresh the hurt is, you should try to talk things out instead of bearing a useless burden and clogging your mind.

Don't go into the reconciliation process with a bitter heart. That will only make the dialogue process difficult. Healthy communication is paramount for you to reach a sensible solution; if not, your discussion may be hostile. Most of the process will involve listening to the other party's grievances and understanding how you hurt them. There will be apologies and a call to forgiveness, then a final resolution.

Keep an open mind while discussing and resolving issues. When you dwell on your hurt, your perspective begins to feel like the only true angle, but this is not true at all. Be flexible and see things from another person's perspective. Put yourself in other people's shoes. Ask yourself questions, such as:

- What exactly made this person get angry and say what he or she said?

- What actions or words of yours were misinterpreted and taken the wrong way?
- Is there a possibility you've interpreted the situation in the wrong way?

Be flexible enough to challenge your own point of view. Rigidity does not help you in your empathy, it only clings to its own beliefs, even when they are incorrect and unhelpful. Compromise your stance for the sake of your friendships.

b. Forgiveness

They might never ask for forgiveness, but forgive anyway. This is for your sake as well, not just the other person's. The more people you vow not to forgive, the more files and tabs are open in the browser of your mind. Imagine how slow your computer would be, if it was invested in so many needless things as your mind. It is time to close some tabs! Clinging to all that trash only makes you suffer. Free yourself now!

Forgiveness doesn't mean you're playing the fool and allowing someone to come into your life and hurt you again. Forgiveness is letting go of all resentment and anger so you are no longer holding onto poison. Forgiveness is hard to give when the other party still hasn't taken responsibility for their actions. Understand that they are on a lower level of understanding and there is no need to stoop so low or act on their level.

CHAPTER FIVE – THE SECRETS OF FINANCIAL MINIMALISM

As new as it may sound to you, financial minimalism is a real concept, and it comes with real benefits. Some of us might have even practiced it without knowing that we were being financially minimalistic. While most of us focus on decluttering our homes and our physical environment, minimalism can also be applied to financial health. All the times you restrained yourself from spending extravagantly, that was financial minimalism. Enrolling in a cashless economy is financial minimalism.

Budgeting, which is a major aspect of financial minimalism, will give more clarity on your spending and help you with your financial priorities. Financial minimalism is not about spending less money, but about only spending money when you need to. It advocates against spending whenever you feel like it. Financial minimalism is about spending intentionally, keeping control of every penny, and not letting any amount slip through your fingers.

How Minimalism Can Help You Financially

1. Financial minimalism helps you to minimize your spending

With financial minimalism, you're only going to purchase the items or services that mean the most to you. Once you have set your purchasing priorities straight, you will naturally have more control over your spending habits. The way you spend money changes when you are focused on acquiring specific items and not just living on a spur-of-the-moment basis. When you spend more intentionally, you naturally begin to save more money.

2. Less excess in your home

Once you are able to control your spending, you automatically control the accumulation of excess in your life. Financial minimalism helps you keep track of the things you already own so you don't continue to buy the same thing, creating clutter. You'll see the results of your intentional spending in the space you live in. Over time, less clutter will form and you'll manage your space far more easily.

3. Gives you more focus for your financial goals

Financial minimalism helps you understand the importance of a financial budget. You spend with a plan, with an aim. Budgeting helps to streamline your spending based on your current needs. It will also help you to identify areas where you have to change the way you handle money. With less money coming out of your accounts, it's much easier to keep your financial goals in sight.

4. Freedom from debt

A good way to simplify your financial life is to get out of debt. In fact, it's difficult to get control over your finances if you still have a lot of debt. Debt can have the same effect on your finances as negative thinking does on your mind. With financial minimalism, it will be easy for you to pinpoint the factors that lead to debt accumulation and tackle them. And on top of this, you will be in a much better position to pay off debt now that you're saving more money due to your new minimalist lifestyle.

5. Giving becomes easier for you

When you have more financial security, you're able to give more without restriction. You're spending less on yourself, so you can give to others when they need it. When you practice financial minimalism, it is easier for you to recognize what and how much of it you can give. While budgeting for the month, you can cut down on some expenses and donate the extra money instead. That way you keep track of your money and know that nothing was wasted.

Minimalist Tips to Help You Achieve Financial Freedom

1. Identify your financial values

You must know the things that are important to you when it comes to money. It will be difficult for you to gain control over your finances if you haven't understood your values yet. Have a clear picture of the money habits in your life that needs to be eliminated. Pick out those that need to be adopted and work on assimilating them into your habits. Discover what your financial values are and start streamlining your budget to suit them. Some practices that you can adopt are:

- Never living above your means
- Eliminating the propensity to borrow
- Sticking to a budget
- Having an emergency fund

With these new practices in your life, it will be easier for you to cut out the non-essentials among your spending. Your financial goals will be reached with less stress and life becomes even simpler.

2. Have an emergency fund

Having an emergency fund is always a lifesaver. The amount you deposit into it will depend on how much you earn, and no matter how small your income is, make sure that a percentage of it goes into the emergency fund. Transfer money into your emergency fund and then carry on with the rest of the month. Don't think of it as another source of money for whenever you want to spend. As its name suggests, it is reserved for emergencies. You have to practice thorough discipline if you want to be successful with it. Whenever you have to take from it, make sure you add more money into it later to maintain a reasonable balance.

3. **Employ digital help**

There are many fantastic apps in the app store that will help you pay your bills automatically without causing you any stress. All you need is to input your payment method, the scheduled time for the payment, and the amount to be paid. A few days before the payment is to be made, you will be alerted about the incoming deductions. Some of these apps will also help you keep track of how much you spent on a particular service over a period of time. By making full use of these apps, you never have to worry about making a payment on time (and potentially creating debt!), and you save a little bit of time every month.

4. **Develop a budgeting system that works and stick to it**

Do you want to spend less than you make? Then the solution is simple: you need a budget. Budgeting helps you to manage expenses and never spend more than you can afford. Regardless of how much you make, the money that leaves your hands every month should never be more than what comes in; if it is, you stand a risk of running into more debt. It sounds like something everyone should be able to do easily, but this isn't the case at all.

Group your expenses into categories to help you keep track of how much you spend on each category. Keep the categories as consolidated as possible, so the list doesn't grow too long. Common categories include utilities, phone bills, transportation, rent, food, and miscellaneous. The contents of the list will differ from person to person due to various reasons, but they should share streamlined equality. Brainstorm and estimate how much you spend for each category per month and use that to create your final budget.

It is one thing to have a budget; it is another thing to stick to it. Don't create a budget for the sake of creating a budget. Resist the urge to sit back and suddenly feel that everything is going to be okay. Your work is not done! Discipline should bind you to your budget. Temptations will arise and try to surface your old habits, so prepare yourself for this. Keep your focus on your core financial values, and you will always come out successful.

5. **Minimize debt**

Simply put, "Debt is money stolen from your future savings." And who said time travel wasn't a thing, when people are stealing from their future selves every day. You can always find the discipline to prevent yourself from falling into debt, no matter how tight the situation may seem. Seek out other options. Shift your mentality towards owning things that you can afford at the present moment, instead of buying things on credit and insisting you'll get your act together later. The peace of mind that comes from having no debt is far more rewarding than the fleeting high your spur-of-the-moment purchase gave you.

6. **Find the best deals**

Whenever you need to purchase something, take your time to research and find the best deals around. It may take a little bit of time, but the end result is worth it. You'll still get the exact same thing, but you'll be spending less money. Don't be so hasty to spend your hard-earned dollars just because you can afford it. Saving some money by finding the best deal will leave you with more money after the transaction. You can put this towards your savings or purchase something else that you need. You'll be amazed by the number of discounts offered. You just have to find them. And remember, although you should go for the best deal, make sure it is still for a high or above-average quality product.

7. **Get rid of distractions**

Think deeply and try to identify all the potential distractions from your financially minimalist life. What are the temptations that push you to buy things that you do not need? If you're subscribed to a particular store that always sends you compelling articles that lead you to buy their products, then unsubscribe. Unfollow social media influencers that are constantly tempting you into buying new products you don't need. If there is something or someone in your life, making you feel like your life is incomplete, remove that trigger. You won't be sorry and you won't be lesser for it. With these distractions out of the way, you can finally focus all your attention on doing right by your finances and your life.

CHAPTER SIX - ADVANCED HOME DECLUTTERING

Now it's time for you to put all your new decluttering skills to work. In this chapter, we will be going through the various rooms in the house. I will be providing you with some tips on how to get rid of the excess in these rooms and defeat clutter instantly. Start from the room that feels most comfortable to you or the room with the most clutter. It is your call. Just make sure you actually begin the process and keep up with it. You don't have to follow the exact order I am going to detail here. At this point, the decluttering principles we studied in chapter three will be very important. Use them to guide you through the decluttering process of each room. The tips in this chapter will only be the basics.

A Room-by-Room Decluttering Guide
1.   LIVING ROOM

First, visualize your living room as you want it. Identify the furniture you want to keep and the ones that you will leave. Figure out all the things that should be on the shelves and the surface spaces.

Next, begin to ditch all of those things that will hinder your living room from being the perfect living room. Purging unnecessary items one day at a time will make a dramatic impact and transform your sitting-room within days. Consider the values that each item brings into the general sitting-room ambiance. Ask yourself questions about each item. Do the decorative objects really provide the joy and satisfaction that have been attributed to their presence? Have they become too old and outdated? Are they a little worn? And most importantly, do you even like them or are they gifts you just feel you *have to* like?

Send everything into its space. Figure out the areas to store your DVDs, games, and computer. Make sure that every other object in the sitting-room is kept in their appropriate area. All surfaces should remain clear, and stray objects should not be found on surfaces that do not belong to them. The surfaces in question include coffee tables, side tables, and desks. The sitting room floor should be kept tidy too.

Set a limit for the number of furniture and decorative materials that will exist in the sitting-room at any given time. Limit the things collected into the sitting-room. Display fewer items so that attention doesn't get divided and clutter doesn't begin to form again. This is the space in which you will be receiving guests, so stay aware of the impression your sitting-room is leaving on people who visit you.

2. **BEDROOM**

The bedroom is one of the most cluttered parts of the house. Since it's one of the more private rooms in the house, we think that we can do anything here and it won't matter. It does matter. Maybe not to your guests, but it is affecting your ability to rest in this room.

Before you begin to declutter, take a moment to picture what you want your bedroom to look like after the decluttering process. What kind of room do you envision? Begin to remove all the things creating clutter.

You should select items to keep, donate or trash. You will come across items that should be taken out of the room to another room where they will serve more important purposes. Sort them into their own pile and take them out later, to be arranged in their new home.

Dividing the bedroom into zones is quite easy. There will be a space for sleeping, dressing, and, for some, working. Sort the things in the room into their various spaces and organize them neatly. Keep the things you will need most often very close to you, somewhere on your bedside table.

Deal with surfaces and plan out the items that should be found on them every day. The bed is the most important surface in the room, and it is necessary for your wellbeing. It should always be kept as clear, clean, and organized as possible. Eliminate all clutter that is forming on your bed. You should also organize your wardrobe so it will be easier to handle your clothes and prevent them from finding their way onto the bed.

3. **KITCHEN**

The kitchen is the powerhouse of the home. If it is in disarray, everybody in the home feels it. There will be missing cutlery, broken ceramics, wafts of dust underneath the cabinets and pests in every corner. Since perishables and food are kept in this room, you must keep this space clean. Otherwise, you may start to attract unwelcome little guests, in the form of rodents or cockroaches. Due to its significance, the kitchen is filled with a lot of appliances and other tools. Once the objects in this room build into a clutter, the functionality of this space becomes undermined.

The beauty of every kitchen is in its spaciousness and the availability of clear countertops. That is what makes it desirable to cook here. Think about how lovely it will be to have your cabinets and shelves organized in the most welcoming way.

The first thing to do is empty every single cabinet or shelf in the kitchen. Even if you are sure that you will be returning an item back to this space, remove it still. You might not know how much space it is taking up just by being in that spot. Plus, removing everything provides the opportunity to clean the cabinet.

Sort through the items and find those that should be kept, donated, or trashed. When was the last time you used a particular appliance? Is it even working still? With each item you pick, ask yourself these important questions that will help you reach a conclusion about the future of each item.

If you have never categorized the items in your kitchen, you should do that now. Break them into groups such as baking items, cutting tools, everyday appliances, and mugs. Find all excess and drop them into the donation box.

Tips for Getting Rid of Sentimental Clutter

Some sentimental objects are worth keeping. Like a deceased relative's fur coat or a prized antique, but let's face it, there are some sentimental things that need to go. Do you really need your ex-boyfriend's old guitar picks? Or your mother's (no matter how deceased she may be) incredibly ugly old mugs? Probably not. Even if you know you don't want them or need them, they can still be hard to get rid of. Keep these tips in mind:

- **Eliminate all guilt**

Sometimes we don't throw away sentimental objects because we feel guilty. Think about where this guilt stems from. Is the object in question something that once belonged to an old relative? Do you feel bad because it's like you're throwing away a piece of them? Nip this thinking in the bud. People are not their possessions. Chances are you have something else from them that is far more useful and that doesn't create as much clutter. You are not harming anyone here, so don't feel guilty.

- **Focus on a different aspect of the memory**

Another reason why we keep sentimental things is because they are attached to a certain memory. This makes total sense. Luckily for you, you don't have to throw away the memory if you throw away the object. If you're throwing away an item connected to a memory, consider writing a journal entry about the memory instead. Immortalize it that way. Or look at old pictures of this memory. Let's say you're holding onto your mother's ugly mugs because she used to drink her favorite coffee out of them. Well, hold on a sec, you also live in the house where your mother used to drink her favorite coffee out of her ugly mugs. See the kitchen as the connection to this memory instead.

- **Give it to someone else**

If you know someone else who might want this item, consider giving it to them. This way, you don't have to see the object in the garbage. Someone out there still has it and still appreciates it. And if the object is something that belongs to someone else in the first place (like an ex-boyfriend), then give it back already! There's no use holding on.

The Best Way to Decorate and Design a Minimalist Home

When decorating your minimalist home, you should keep three important factors in mind:

a. Quality
b. Spaciousness
c. Clear surfaces

These factors are more important than the subjective beauty of your decorative items. By keeping these factors in mind, almost any decorative item can look appealing. Use these tips to get started:

1.   Go for neutral colours

Riots of color can sometimes appear as clutter. Try to keep your color combinations as simple and neutral as possible. Go for colors that inspire a feeling of calmness, whatever that means to you. It may not be the same color for everyone, but it's rarely bright or neon color. It doesn't mean that you cannot experiment with colors and get creative; it just means you should first study the colors you want, think about how those colors affect you and find out if they work well together. Ask yourself if the combination is easy on the eyes. Remember, this is your private, resting space. It's absolutely vital that you can relax here.

2. Quality over quantity

You should consider each piece carefully before you let it into your home. Work with few objects while decorating your home, but make sure that every single object is of a reasonable or high quality. Your goal is to create a comfortable space that anyone would be comfortable in. Choose well-made designs that are built to last. Since you will be using these objects a lot, it is important that they will survive more than a few uses.

3. Bring in nature

Florals and greenery will add a beautiful touch of nature to your sitting-room and kitchen. The colors from flowers or other plants will also add to the overall color scheme of your home. Keep this in mind when you are choosing your natural pieces. What's wonderful about plants is they bring in so much beauty and they last as long as you are able to take care of them. Hopefully, that is a long time! Be good to your plants.

4. Interesting accessories

The accessories in a room can change the entire look of the room. An accessory in this regard is anything that is added to a room to give it an aesthetic value. Throw in one or two well-selected accessories or decorations such as wall art, mirrors, candles, picture frames and rugs. Work with variety but try to maintain balance even as you work this into your space.

5. Keep it simple

The beauty of minimalism is in its simplicity. Adopt the 'less is more' approach to your interior décor. Continue to keep space in mind as you work. Your space doesn't have to be boring. In fact, minimalist decorations when done well can be far more beautiful than hordes of decorations staring at you from every corner. Just take it one step at a time and make sure to be fully committed to minimalist aesthetics.

CHAPTER SEVEN - DIGITAL DECLUTTERING

Since the world went digital, our lives have become more comfortable, we have become more productive, and information dissemination is now faster. But there is a downside: we have also become obsessed with electronics and digital devices. The devotion we show these little gadgets has reached an alarming stage. Things that were produced for us to control have now gradually become our masters.

Here is a quick picture: hours on social media, hundreds of unread emails in our inboxes, a desktop littered with folders and files, storage devices filled with hundreds or even thousands of photos, music, and videos. It is overwhelming, to say the least. We never knew it would happen until digital clutter became an important topic.

Since we spend most of our time in the digital world, doesn't it make sense to keep our digital lives decluttered as well? Doesn't it make sense to keep our devices, which make our lives so much easier, as smooth-functioning as possible? How much of the things (documents, files, and folders) saved up in your digital space do you actually need? When did you last do a cleanup of your phone or computer?

Apart from the clutter on our digital devices, there is also clutter that can form from our overdependence on these devices. We spend hours plugged into these gadgets that they now define our happy and sad moments. Shut down your computer or phone and do something more physically or mentally demanding. Even if you work from a laptop most of the time, set out at least one hour per day to do something different like reading a book, taking a walk, talking to another human or even talking to yourself. Live in the real world, not just the digital world.

The Principles of Digital Minimalism

- **Your devices should make your life easier not harder**

That's why they were invented in the first place, after all. Our phone and our computer should be helping our lives function more smoothly, with more ease. They should be helping us navigate obstacles, not creating more. You're not living by this principle if you find huge chunks of your time taken up by your device. Consider if the time you spend on your device is more than the time saved through its functional features.

- **Usage of your device should be intentional not addictive**

How often do you pick up your phone out of habit and anxiety, and not because you mean to carry out a specific action? There's a difference between opening your device to send an email and opening your device because you need to do something, anything, with your hands. Try to only use your device if there is something very specific you need it for.

- **Always put people before machines**

This one should be a given, but it's not, to so many people. We always think we're connecting with people because we're talking to them on the internet; while that's true sometimes, we also tend to ignore the people that are right in front of us to do this. Is your addiction to your phone getting in the way of your everyday interactions? How many times do you find yourself scrolling while you're in the company of someone who is trying to talk to you? Never let your machines take over.

Important Advice for Defeating Digital Clutter

1. **E-mails**: A cluttered inbox is enough to overwhelm you, when all you're trying to do is check up on your latest messages. The problem worsens when you have multiple emails for different purposes. If that is the case, then take it one email at a time.

First, go through the different categories (your inbox, outbox, drafts, sent mail, etc.) and delete everything you do not need a record of. It is a tedious job, but it is worth it. You will find mail that has been there for years and mail that you replied to a long time ago. Work on your contact lists. Which services send you the most emails and why? Do you find the emails helpful in any way or do they just drive you to purchase things you don't need? If this adds to clutter, then unsubscribe, block, or delete.

Adopt a new habit of checking through your mail once in the morning and once in the evening, instead of doing so at random intervals. This way, digital clutter doesn't build up. Declutter your inbox of unnecessary emails every day so that clutter doesn't begin to build up again. Each week, run through your sent emails and delete those that need to be deleted. Cultivate these habits and practices, and make sure you don't fall back into old habits of ignoring digital clutter in your electronic mail.

2. **Social Media:** Social media clutter can manifest itself in a variety of ways. First, there is an accumulation of unnecessary friends and people on your 'following' list. Sometimes you go online and see posts from people that you barely remember how you met. Sometimes you may feel this blanket of guilt coming over you as you unfriend or delete some contacts, but there is no good reason for this. This is a healthy habit for your digital life. There is no need to keep in contact with someone you barely know, especially if what they post is annoying or irrelevant to your life. Delete them and don't feel bad,

Cleaning up your social media accounts on various platforms will help set your priorities straight and feed you with relevant information, pictures, and status updates that you actually care about. Your mind also benefits from this because it will have lesser visual clutter to deal with, and it can focus on what you like.

The same method can be applied across all social media platforms. Streamline all your subscriptions and follow the necessary pages. Connect your accounts across platforms to make your internet experience flow with ease.

Lastly, don't get consumed by social media. These platforms, even with all their numerous benefits, eat your time up. Don't spend more than ten minutes at a time on each platform. Do what you have come to do and leave. You are only allowed to spend more time than normal if you are running a Twitter advocacy group or making money from running Facebook ads. If it doesn't benefit you emotionally, mentally, or financially then you have no reason to spend more than an hour per day scrolling through an app.

3. **YOUR COMPUTER OR LAPTOP**

Most computer systems are digital junkyards. Is yours one of those? Only you can answer. The decluttering process starts by cleaning up your desktop. Think about your desktop as your parking lot or driveway. It is an introduction to your digital home. In fact, by merely looking at the level of organization on some desktops, I can tell how organized the owners are. There are many desktop icons that you don't use. Delete them: shortcuts, folders, and files. If there are documents that you still feel will be important to you in the future, you have the option of backing it up on cloud storage. But be careful, so your cloud storage doesn't suffer from clutter transfer. Only back up the files that you will definitely need in the future.

Minimalism & Decluttering

Keep all icons arranged at the left side of the desktop and ensure that they don't take up more than three rows at a time. If there are files that you reopen occasionally, put them in a folder and name them. Sort everything on your desktop by type.

Next, uninstall any programs that you rarely use. Free up space on your hard drive so your system can operate smoothly. Ensure that every single application installed on your system is one that is used frequently, not just eating space for no reason.

Focus on categorizing your documents into relevant folders so that it will be easier to find each of them when they are needed. You will need concentration for this one and perhaps a pen and book to jot down the name of each new folder and the files in them. With your documents neatly organized in your computer, it will be easier for you to navigate through your system. The goal is to get through each folder and get rid of the excess and unnecessary documents.

Maintain the decluttered state of your computer by constantly deleting unnecessary files you don't need. Become a gatekeeper and keep track of all downloaded files. Keep them organized in the download folder so they can be deleted easily when the time comes.

CHAPTER EIGHT - PERFECTING THE MINIMALISM EXPERIENCE

Minimalism is not just a lifestyle; it is an experience. Everything that we do contributes to the overall journey. These are the experiences that you should seek out, the experiences you should spend your money when you're not spending on useless stuff. Possessions and property gratify the body while worthy experiences delight the soul and mind. The nourishment of the soul and mind is important for the wellbeing of the body. That is why it is impossible to be attracted to an insane person, no matter how beautiful their bodies look.

Stocking our lives and homes with the latest gadgets seems satisfying because it provides you with the thrill of a brand new purchase, but this only lasts for a short period. The thrill dies off, and you are left in the same place you once found yourself: searching for another item to give you the same thrill. The cycle goes on, and you're never more satisfied than you were before. There are better ways for you to spend your money.

Why We Need Experiences More Than Material Things

Money spent on experience is money spent nurturing the soul. The joy gotten from experiences lasts longer than the fleeting joy from purchasing stuff. This is why:

   a. **Experiences help to solidify your own purpose and passions**

Everything that you do and spend money on should influence your future and propel you towards your purpose and passions in life; material possessions rarely compel you to do this. If you're obsessed with mountaineering, owning a hundred books on the topic or a dozen mountaineering outfits can never be equated to actually going on a mountaineering expedition. Material possessions will only fuel your imagination in regards to the experience, but the experience is what actually fuels your soul and satisfies you. This is why people go on road trips to see the country for themselves, not through pictures. This is why people go to music festivals; to see their favorite artists perform in person and not just listen to the same old recording.

b. **Shared experiences can foster relationships**

An experience shared is a part of you shared. It's as simple as that. It is a bond that remains as long as both parties are alive. Have you ever caught yourself just smiling because the memory of a shared experience has come to your mind? It is a wonderful feeling, isnt it? Experiences shared with people made them closer to you. Think about all the close friendships you have and try to figure out what makes the friendship strong. The chances are high that those friendships blossomed over time because of a powerful shared experience or a series of shared experiences. Once you meet up with people you have shared your experiences with, there is never a dull moment. There are plenty of memories shared between the two parties, and conversations can last hours.

c. **Experiences introduce you to new things**

A life without new experiences is a boring life devoid of learning and expansion of the mind Experiences can teach you the importance of life and friendship, and they can give you a changed, brand new perspective on the world. Everyone who has ever experienced real and transformative change did so because of one singular experience. Everyday people are discovering their purpose in life because of experiences, something they would have never known if they had chased possessions instead.

d. **Craving experiences will eliminate worries associated with buying stuff**

In an earlier chapter, we established the degree of anxiety and worry that comes with purchasing new stuff. What if I was ripped off? What if I get robbed? What if this iPhone I bought for $999 suddenly drops into a bucket of water? The 'what ifs' are numerous and they make you paranoid. It takes up so much mental energy that you become stressed. That is not to say that you should never buy new things and spoil yourself once in a while, but seeking out experiences will greatly reduce these worries. Once you have some money saved up and have gotten your supplies ready, you can make plans and go after any experiences without worry. Your experience can never be taken away from you. Once you get it, it is yours forever, unlike all your material possessions.

Experiences that are Better Than Any Material Object You Can Buy

1. Travel

How long have you remained in the current city or town you live in? A lot of people are comfortable staying in one place for more than a decade without crossing the borders. Just because your place of worship, a shopping mall, school, library and possibly a cinema are available where you reside doesn't mean there's no reason to venture out. Social media has made this situation worse since you can stay in your room and feel like you've traveled across the world through the internet. But there is more to the world than the city you live in. Go out and see for yourself. Don't depend on the pictures.

The feeling of being in a different country, experiencing their culture, and learning their stories is unparalleled. You can eat their local cuisine and learn a new language. You can even travel to the next city and take pictures of beautiful sights on your way there. Visit a relative and spend the night with them. Store the memories from your journeys and expand your mind. You need not travel far; just travel somewhere.

2. Festivals

Festivals bring passionate and excited people from everywhere to engage in a shared experience. Going to festivals with your friends is a great way to bond and meet new people. Even if you get lost and wander to the other side of the festival grounds, there is always a new experience waiting for you. Most of the people that go to festivals are people that share the same passions as you and meeting them will ignite your passion with even brighter flames.

Festivals are filled with culture, life, music, art, and people. There is always something to captivate you, no matter your interests are. Festivals are events where you can be yourself and express your individuality, no matter how weird. There are so many kinds of festivals you can enjoy. Music festivals are by far the most common, but there are also literary festivals and cultural festivals. Try them all!

3. A Weekend Getaway with Friends

You can plan this. All you need to do is to pick a location and travel there with friends. The main thing here is not the destination, but the journey itself. Arriving at your intended location will be fun too, but there's also nothing like getting together with friends and the laughter you share along the way. You don't even have to spend the night, wherever it is you travel to. You can go there in the morning, spend some time and be back by dinnertime.

For example, if you have friends who are art enthusiasts, you can plan to go to a museum or an art exhibition. Savor your experience by allowing yourself to be fully engaged in the program at hand. Or you could go on a hiking trip with friends and you could even camp out in the woods, if you're the outdoorsy type.

The beauty of going on such trips is the uncertainty that awaits you. You never know who or what you will meet, the humor you will find, or the stories that will be shared and created. These are the experiences from which life is truly made. One day, when you think back on your life, this is what you will remember.

4. Learn something new and exciting

The process of introducing your mind to something new will enhance the quality of your life and refine your mind. Your confidence levels will see a boost once you have success with your learning process. As we get older, our minds weaken because we no longer approach new activities or challenges with the same zest of our younger years. This is because we feel more tired and less motivated, not because we are less capable. The mind is always in search of new things to delve deeply into. If you keep on feeding it with routine or the same old information you already know, it keeps on getting weaker and loses its ability to stretch outwards.

It is also incredibly fun to learn new things. Don't see it as an activity you are 'bad' at, but an activity that you can learn from, that can show you a whole new side of the world. So many possibilities open up to you when you decide to grab the bull by the horns and learn something exciting. The process of discovery is filled with so much excitement. It can also be unexpectedly rewarding; you may find that your newfound skills open doors to a promotion or a new vocation entirely.

The Experiences that Make Far Better Gifts than 'Stuff'

We're so attached to the expectation of showing up with a material object in hand, wrapped and ribbon-tied, ready to be opened. The world has fed us the idea that this is what we need to do to celebrate someone. We need a physical representation of our joy, our celebratory spirit. It's time to change this approach. There are many experiences we can gift our loved ones that are far more fun or special than a material object. They may even like it a lot more. Think of the clutter in your home, that heap of stuff that consists of bad gifts that you can't throw away. Don't add to someone else's clutter pile! Consider gifting these experiences:

1. Cooking Classes

Not only do cooking classes teach you valuable skills, they are also incredibly fun! Cooking without having to clean up afterwards? Yes, please! There are classes that teach a range of different cuisines. For something fun, baking desserts is always a great choice. Look online to find classes in your area.

2. A Spa Day or In-Home Massage

Why get someone a bottle of lotion or fragrant oil when you can buy them the experience of someone actually using it on them? It's a far better gift, if you ask me. Purchase a gift card for a local spa or arrange to have a masseuse come to their house. Everyone loves to feel pampered.

3. A Concert Ticket

Whoever it is you're buying a gift for definitely has a favorite musician or artist. See if this singer or band is on tour in the state any time soon. Oftentimes people miss this opportunity because they never think to check if their favorite artist is on tour. Even if they're absolute favorite will not be playing, something similar will also be enjoyable.

4. A Restaurant Gift Card

Many fabulous restaurants offer gift cards for this exact purpose. Treat someone you know to a fantastic dinner. Everyone enjoys a fantastic meal, especially when they aren't paying for it. This gift will not create clutter and it will fill their bellies.

5. Tickets to a Play or Musical

What's wonderful about this gift is that everyone enjoys theatre, but people will rarely buy themselves tickets to a performance. Yet once you're there, you get swept up in what an enthralling experience it is. You always enjoy it more than you think you will. Gift someone this experience because they are bound to have a great time.

6. Yoga Classes

Many yoga studios or instructors will offer a set number of classes for a discounted price. Consider treating someone you know to body-nourishing yoga, especially if you think exercise will benefit them. When someone buys us a gift, we feel like we have to make good use of it or they'll bad. Take advantage of this for something that will truly benefit your friend or relative!

7. Rosetta Stone

One of the best ways to learn a new language is with the program Rosetta Stone. If you know your friend or relative has a fascinating with a particular culture or country, gift them the experience of learning the language of that place. People rarely think to do this, but once they are given the opportunity, they are grateful for it.

8. Membership Programs

This may sound vague, but that's only because of just how much there is to choose from. When you gift someone a membership program, you are expanding their lifestyle. Get them a gym or museum membership. Or perhaps, a yearly pass to their favorite national park or amusement park. Most of these places allow you to buy a yearly pass. One thing is for sure: everyone will love this gift.

9. Free Babysitting

Do you know someone with kids they desperately need a break from? Offer them free babysitting sessions. You could write this out on a card or piece of paper and make it look like an official ticket. Commit to any number of sessions that you think you can handle, e.g. two or three sessions will help a lot but will also prevent you from becoming overwhelmed. It's an unconventional gift but any tired parent will deeply appreciate this.

10. A Staycation

Why not?! If you know someone who needs to take time out to unwind and feel pampered, pay for a night at a local hotel. Ideally, it should be somewhere comfortable and beautiful. It should be somewhere they'll enjoy more than home. When we get out of our space, we feel more relaxed. I know for sure that one of your friends needs this. Consider gifting a staycation experience!

Conclusion

Congratulations on finishing this book! I know the ideas and information I've presented to you have inspired you to begin the decluttering process of your home. The message of minimalism is not preached often, but it should be. Wouldn't you agree? We live in a consumerist world, and some people even frown upon minimalism; don't allow their attitudes to influence you. Protect your minimalist mindset at all costs. Do not allow the things you have learned throughout this book to slip your mind. Once you finish this book, you may even come across an ad telling you to buy a new product right now. Before you consider making this purchase, remember these companies don't really care about you. They just want to sell their product, and they'll tell you anything to make that happen. You are the cow they are trying to milk.

The journey of minimalism is never an easy one. You will come across people who loathe or even despise you for living by a different philosophy. They do so out of their own ignorance. And there is little you can do about it, especially when they aren't willing to hear you out. It is only natural. We, humans, are always quick to condemn things we do not understand. People will jump to conclusions and suggest that you aren't materialistic simply because you are unsuccessful. Of course, you and I know that isn't the case. By now, you've come to a complete understanding of how our quality of life is not determined by how much we own. In fact, clutter and excess can get in the way of our emotional, mental, or professional progress - the real things that contribute to our quality of life.

As I said in the preceding chapters, find your tribe, the people that share your minimalist goals with you. In recent years the conversation about minimalism and decluttering has increased exponentially. Join the conversation on social media and fuel your drive. You will need all the encouragement you can get. You will certainly come across people who have struggled with the things you are struggling with now. They will help you out with any questions you may have, especially now that our journey in this book has come to an end.

The benefits of minimalism are numerous, as I have stated before: freedom from clutter, financial security, and above all, peace of mind. This freedom allows you to chase experiences with a deeper meaning and greater relevance to your goals. You will discover yourself for who you truly are and not what you own. Your confidence will see a big boost because you no longer depend on your possessions and property to determine your value.

It is up to you now. We have gone through all of the most important facets of minimalism: the major habits, the principles, decluttering procedures, tips to reduce mental, emotional, and digital declutter, and much more. It is now up to you to keep practicing and building your great minimalist habits until they come naturally to you. Discipline and consistency are the most important factors in practicing minimalism. Never let go of them. Stay alert of clutter monsters and starve them to death before they become a huge menace. I wish you luck on your minimalist journey!

Improve Money Management by Learning the Steps to a Minimalist Budget

Learn How to Save Money, Control your Personal Finances, Avoid Consumerism, Invest Wisely and Spend on What Matters to You

Table of Contents

Introduction 101

Chapter 1 – The Minimalist Budget Mindset 104

How to dramatically shift your thinking from a negative to positive mindset when it comes to money 106

Free yourself from a Consumerist Mindset 112

Quick Start Action Steps to free yourself from Compulsive Spending once and for all 118

Chapter 2 - Start Saving Money 126

Figure out where the heck all your money goes every month ... 126

Steps to track your expenses 127

11 simple ways to instantly start saving money 130

How to develop self-discipline to stop yourself from overspending 138

Chapter 3 - Budgeting Strategies and Financial Plans 147

4 powerful budgeting strategies to align your spending with your money-saving goals 149

Making sure that budget strategy implementation is successful 152

15 Easy steps to come up with a financial plan that lets you save more and earn more 153

Chapter 4 - Get out of debt 162

Find out what causes debt 163

11 practical techniques to help you get out of debt - regardless of the amount 169

Chapter 5 - Make more with less **177**

Learn how to maximize the use of your income 177

Can you live on half your income and save the rest? Probably. 180

Get the information you need to start investing 186

The information you need to start building your personal assets 190

What's the difference between trading and investing? 196

How to make successful investments and get big rewards 197

Conclusion **201**

Introduction

The Minimalist Budget Mindset is a guide to help you save money, spend less and live more efficiently with a minimalist lifestyle.

M0st people approach budgeting with a deflated spirit and they see it as an impossible thing to achieve. They imagine that budgeting will only give them discomfort and strain. Sometimes even without making the effort, they think they are wholly incompatible with budgeting of any kind.

This book will give you a different approach to budgeting. It's truly unfortunate that the idea of living within your means should be experienced as such a deficit. It brings, after all, an abundance of benefits that most are unaware of. You'll soon see what we mean. This book will show you that when you live a minimalist lifestyle and budget accordingly, you can free yourself from the constraints of the modern world. You can say goodbye to financial problems and pervading feelings of denial. No longer will you be overwhelmed by desires that never seem to give you any satisfaction.

A minimalist budget is an approach to self-fulfillment and abundance that might seem counter-intuitive to most. This book will offer the bigger picture of what it means to budget. You will realize there is more to it than money management. You will also learn that when a life budget considers your behavioral, emotional, social and spiritual capital, you will make much better decisions.

We will talk about spending and shopping habits, identify problem areas, explore debt and how you can achieve your financial goals. You will look at ways you can put these principles into place and ensure that you stay motivated and focused. This book emphasizes the concept of minimalism instead of thriftiness. You aren't buying cheaply, you are minimizing the impulse to buy unnecessarily. That's right, even your cheap purchases need to go. They're doing more harm than you think!

If you can create a budget with a better understanding of your relationship with money and how it affects your lifestyle, the changes you apply will be long-lasting and truly authentic.

Minimalism isn't about surviving with less than you need. It's about identifying what you need and fulfilling the need completely without accumulating excess. Having exactly what you need is far from suffering. In fact, the excess in your life is responsible for more suffering than you even realize. Minimalist budgeting is about knowing what you need to have enough, and how best you can use your money to achieve that. When you approach your finances with this mindset, every penny is used efficiently and nothing is wasted.

We live a short life, and material goods and money can provide us with new ways to enjoy our life. They can assist us in moving closer to what we find worthwhile and meaningful. But that doesn't mean that they are worthwhile and meaningful in themselves. How we spend our money is an expression of what we think is crucial and our values, but in no way does it dictate the value or quality of our life. It gives us the illusion of determining our quality of life, and that's the problem. We are measuring happiness and satisfaction by the wrong standards – that's why we never feel we score very high.

How much would you be willing to pay for the calm and peace of mind achieved through living well? How much of your life do you lose when working? When it comes to expenses, do you remember to consider the time you wasted stressing about money? These questions might seem overly philosophical and vague, but they help us get to the root of how we make money, spend it and form a mentality around it. Once we've understood these roots, our efforts to save money will become much easier. We'll develop a more meaningful relationship with money, and this can mean the difference between scraping by and big savings that shape your future.

What will you learn after reading this book? You'll gain a deeper understanding of what makes a long-lasting budget. You will identify crucial and practical saving tips regarding matters of debt, children, cleaning, home, health, clothes, and food. You will also learn how to set realistic goals that match your personal budget. You will learn how to put everything you have learned into practice, come up with your own personal budget and much more.

The longer you cling to your current bad habits, the more difficult it becomes to shift your behavior and thinking. These money-wasting habits take root inside your subconscious and before you know it, it is second nature. To increase the likelihood of succeeding at minimalism and finally make big savings the new norm, it is vital that you start now. Stop wasting time. Stop making excuses. The longer you wait, the longer it is before you finally achieve your goals.

If you want to free yourself from your current financial constraints, then turn the page and read on. The techniques you'll unlock will make lasting, positive changes to your financial standing.

Chapter 1 – The Minimalist Budget Mindset

In recent years, the minimalism trend has become increasingly popular across the United States, particularly among the millennial generation. It has inspired a lot of people to downsize their possessions and live only with what they need. Aside from helping you declutter and destress, adopting a minimalist view of budgeting may also help you achieve financial freedom, releasing you from the shackles of a life lived paycheck to paycheck.

For one to have a minimalist budget, it's crucial to get into a minimalist mindset. It is the mindset of someone who chooses to live a minimalist life and ensure that this mindset becomes the root of all their behavior.

Most people who choose to simplify their life, do so because they begin thinking differently about how they can live a better life. Or perhaps they start to notice the destructive nature of their thoughtless consumerism, leading to a decided effort to make a change.

You need to cultivate the right mindset to ensure that your hard-earned money is spent well. Without the right mindset, the transition into minimalism is a much more difficult endeavor. You will try to resist temptations. You will try to reduce the amount of physical and mental clutter in your life. You will try to look for solutions. But as you try, the inner urges will continue to grow. Without the right mindset, you will find yourself relapsing. Any attempt at minimalism will only have you running back to satisfy your usual desires. This is why mental and emotional preparations are vital.

Minimalist Budget

You may be wary of the idea of unfulfilled desires. This doesn't mean that you should give up on minimalism. In fact, the minimalist budget mindset is not about fighting your desires at all, it's about learning to stop desiring.

When you have cultivated the right mindset, you will realize that it is easy to live a simple life. Your motives will drive you and your actions will fall into place.

The budget mindset is best seen as a reduction of clutter based on your priorities. This doesn't mean you must get rid of or stop buying things that make you happy immediately. Minimization must be done at a reasonable pace. With time, you will begin to only seek out those things that are crucial.

Most people look to cut back on material possessions and objects, but when the minimalist mindset is involved, it applies to relationships and activities as well. After all, many areas of our life can be filled with excess.

Most people don't understand why someone would want to live a life within a minimalist budget. They don't understand how anyone could want to avoid luxuries.

They believe they should live however they want, and that is true. What these people don't understand is that living a minimalist life on a minimalist budget still allows you to do what you want. The things that you want are simply different. Living on a minimalist budget brings many benefits. It's just that most people are not aware of them.

The money mindset encompasses the thoughts and feelings you subconsciously develop toward money from life experiences. Since our thoughts control our actions, developing a negative mindset when it comes to money can create a huge barrier between you and financial health. It can result in stress and anxiety, and it will hinder you from reaching your financial goals.

But developing a negative money mindset doesn't mean you will always feel that way. Read on to learn how you can develop the right mindset to help you achieve your financial goals.

How to dramatically shift your thinking from a negative to positive mindset when it comes to money

Most people know what they're supposed to do when money management is involved – save funds for an emergency, spend less than the money they earn and invest for retirement. But developing other good habits is crucial. Managing money requires discipline and discipline doesn't come automatically; you must learn and teach yourself to abide by your own goals.

Your success in managing money depends on how you think about money. If you want to eliminate financial stress from your life or get better at money management, it's vital that you change how you think about money and develop a positive money mindset. It applies to every aspect of life. You need to make a positive change in everything you do to be successful. This will help you change what and how you talk.

Speaking and thinking more positively will make a huge difference, but it also requires action. It is essential that you change how you've been doing things, and take steps in a new direction for real and lasting change.

During times of hardship, such as after the death or loss of a partner, it can seem challenging to develop a positive mindset about anything. And not just about money. You might experience even more financial difficulties after this loss. Or perhaps you aren't short of money, but you have no knowledge about how to handle your finances, and this makes you nervous about the future.

Stress due to finances can come from anywhere, and it might become worse when grief or trauma are involved.

Fortunately, there are many steps you can take to dramatically shift your mindset from negative to positive, and develop great habits. Here are the steps you can take:

1. Forgive yourself for financial mistakes you've made

You won't find anyone who has never missed a bill or credit card payment. Everyone has spent some of their savings in the spur of the moment. Virtually all adults have made these same mistakes, and that's why you should forgive yourself.

When you forgive yourself for past mistakes, it will set you free. You will make room for a healthy attitude and better practices for saving money. Stop focusing on guilt and start focusing on progress.

2. Know your money mindset

You may think you understand your attitude towards money, but chances are you're not fully aware of how your mindset affects your decision-making. It's recommended that you track the thoughts that cross your mind every time you make a decision concerning money. What type of items do you find yourself reaching for? What problems do you imagine they will solve? What events in your life trigger these desires?

Since we make a lot of these decisions in our lives, you should do this for at least one whole day and examine the results. Look for patterns that give you a clue about your attitude.

Once you come to a better understanding about your mindset, it will be easy to identify habits and beliefs that prevent you from abiding by plans and goals.

3. Don't compare yourself to others

In the age of reality TV, celebrity magazines and social media, it's easy to make comparisons. We compare ourselves to celebrities, friends, family members and even fictional characters on television. You need to quit this bad habit for a few reasons:

- You're comparing what you know about yourself to only what you see of somebody else. What you're comparing yourself to is the best side of someone's life. What you see in the media is carefully curated for the public and in no way reflective of reality.

- You don't know the details of the other people's finances. Some might live a luxurious life, but it's likely many of these people are also paying off credit card debt.

- After comparing yourself to others, you'll be filled with feelings of inadequacy. This will divert attention from your aspirations and finances, slowing further progress.

Therefore, you should create achievable goals, and measure your success this way. Celebrate the wins and keep your goals updated when you achieve them.

4. Create good habits and maintain them

Once you've established realistic goals, it's good to develop the habits that will help you achieve them. If you've never looked at your expenses in detail or created a budget, then perhaps it's time to do so. When you understand how you're spending money, it can be easy to figure out where you can save.

It'll help you create attainable goals which, step by step, will lead you towards success. One effective habit is following a set time to review your finances and check on progress. If you are in a relationship, choose a time that works for both of you and make sure you're both present.

Even if one partner is appointed to be the money manager, ensure that both parties are on the same page and agree to arranged goals to avoid miscommunication. When you have a clear picture of your financial situation, you can discuss how to delegate money.

5. Become a money mindset sponge

One of the easiest ways to build a good money mindset is to surround yourself with people who live by the values you most admire. When you spend time with people that have a good mindset around money, you will actively learn from them, and you will naturally adapt to their qualities over time.

You can also look for free content online as there are a lot of experts that speak on these topics through live streams, podcasts, and YouTube videos. Consider digesting an hour's worth of money mindset content every day.

Taking this simple step will drastically change your perspective and begin eliminating those limiting beliefs that hold you back from achieving your goals. Changing the people that surround you will change your life.

6. Identify your go-to affirmations for daily empowerment

Find five one-liners that you can repeat daily to center yourself, keep you aligned with your financial goals, and inspire you to make leaps towards success.

For instance, if you struggle with the idea that people with money are greedy, then you're likely engaging in subconscious self-sabotage by keeping a low-paying job. The ideal affirmation for you should be a reminder that having money and being a good person are two different things. Keep telling yourself that you'll give back more to the world when you have more money.

If you grew up feeling that money is scarce and that only some people are entitled to it, then you need to remind yourself there's unlimited money and it's coming your way because you deserve it.

Write down powerful affirmations and keep them in places such as your car dashboard, your wallet, on your bathroom mirror or your smartphone lock screen. Keep reading them out loud. It might seem ridiculous at first, but after some time, you'll start to believe them.

Repetition will lead to results, and everything you concentrate on will start to manifest into reality.

7. Ditch negative language

Perhaps you've noticed that most people spend a lot of their time complaining. Sometimes it can be the easiest way to bond with someone, break an awkward silence, or get some cheap gratification.

Most negative conversations revolve around four topics: a bad relationship, work complaints, a bad financial situation, or bad health.

If you engage in these conversations often, you need to stop and concentrate on your dreams. You can't have both excuses and the results at the same time. When you allow unrestricted negative ideas to flow out of your mouth, you can fall into a sense of self-pity and self-victimization. These feelings will prevent you from taking powerful action, and hold you back from your goals.

Eliminate negative language from your self-talk and see everything as an opportunity for growth. Positive language might seem cheesy at first, but it leads to positive beliefs that will attract positive outcomes.

8. Get the right mentors

Think about who you take advice from. Is it your partner? Your parents? Your co-workers? While they may have some interesting insights, they're not always the most helpful mentors.

Challenge yourself to seek advice from those who have already achieved the goals you are trying to achieve. This means you need to get clear about what you want. Do you want your business to make more money? Do you want a new job? Do you want to completely pay off your debt? Don't just seek out those who are close to you; seek out those you are most interested in emulating.

Reflect on what you want, seek out those mentors, and prepare to spend a lot of time learning from them.

9. Practice gratitude

Daily gratitude has proven powerful. You can start by writing down three things you are grateful for each day. Check your gratitude journal every time you are overwhelmed or feeling negative about your finances. This will give you a positive boost. Studies have shown that gratitude practices can actually rewire the brain to feel happiness more often. The more happy you are, the less likely you are to give into your bad spending habits.

10. Learn and implement new knowledge

Being educated on financial matters will help you feel confident and in control of the future. Consider finding the right education for yourself. Different approaches work best for different people. Explore and discover the financial education that suits you best.

You will find books, experts, and educational platforms that offer a range of different approaches. Education is crucial to maintaining a positive money mindset.

Free yourself from a Consumerist Mindset

Most of the world's population has a consumerist mindset. It doesn't just refer to the omnipresence of advertising, but everything related to the idea that we must own more stuff to be better, more successful, or happier people. This mindset is pervasive in today's culture.

We must emphasize that this consumerist belief is not based in any truth. Owning less brings more benefits than owning more. Freedom from a consumerist mindset brings:

- **More freedom from comparison** – You'll be liberated from constant comparisons to other people's lives. No longer will your mind be fraught with envy, looking at what other people have versus what you don't. Constant comparisons can make us depressed and unable to enjoy what we have. Without this in our lives, you'll feel far more secure than you ever have before.

- **More time and opportunities to pursue other things** – Most material things fade, spoil, and perish. But joy, love, purpose, and compassion stand eternal. Our lives are better lived pursuing them. Being less preoccupied with possessions offers this opportunity. Once you clear your life of meaningless objects and expenses, you will have a lot more money and energy to focus on what truly makes you happy.

- **Less debt** – Money that would have gone towards buying pointless new things can now be invested in more important areas of your life. Owning less allows you to finally start saving money and pay off debt.

- **Less stress** – Many people don't realize this, but it can be stressful to own things you no longer use or care about. This can be guilt-induced stress or stress from maintaining the object. Sometimes these useless possessions can even get in the way. The more objects we own, the more stuff we have to break, and the more money we have to spend to maintain or repair the object. Less possessions means less stuff to worry about.

- **Reduced symptoms of depression** – There is evidence to show that consumerism can increase the likelihood of depression and make symptoms worse. This is because consumerism convinces us there's a lack or void that needs to be filled with material goods. This can create feelings of depression, especially since this void does not exist, so nothing we do can change the way we feel. By defending ourselves against the forces that try to create this dissatisfaction, we will feel much more fulfilled in our daily lives. This is who we really are without consumerism in our lives.

- **Gratitude and contentment**– The easiest way to feel satisfied is to appreciate what you have. It's only natural that when you have less, you appreciate what you have even more. You are more likely to care for and maintain belongings when you don't have as much to worry about.

Breaking from compulsive consumerism is an important step towards a simplified life. How, then, do we achieve this freedom? What are the required steps to break free? Here is a helpful guide for achieving freedom from a consumerist mindset.

1. **Admit it's possible**

It's important to break out of the mindset that the way you live now is the only way you can live. Recognize the lifestyle you're used to is only that – the lifestyle you're used to. It is not the lifestyle you need to be happy. A lot of people throughout history adopted a minimalist lifestyle that rejected and overcame consumerism. Find motivation in how these impressive figures did it. This will help you realize that you, too, can find the same success. The journey to victory starts when you admit it's possible.

2. Adopt a traveler's mentality

When traveling, people only take what they need for that journey. This ensures that we feel freer, lighter and more flexible. We pack the essentials we can't live without and we realize that all excess creates more stress down the road.

The adoption of a traveler's mindset has the same benefits for life as it does for travel. You'll feel less weighed down, and yet you'll still have everything you need. A traveler's mindset will also prevent you from spending money on items that are unnecessary.

3. Embrace the benefits of owning less

People don't usually think of the benefits of owning less, but there are many. When these practical benefits are articulated, it becomes easy to understand, recognize and desire. As soon the lifestyle change is made, you can expect to feel inundated with minimalism's benefits, including a stronger sense of lightness and freedom. Instead of focusing on the things you're giving up, start thinking about all the new benefits that will enter your life.

4. Be aware of consumerist tactics

The world will make you believe that the best way to contribute to society is by spending your money. We are swarmed by advertisements every day trying to convince us to buy more and more. Recognizing the consumerist tactics in our world will not make them go away, but they can help you understand when a desire has simply been manufactured by a well-designed advertisement. Many products that are on the market today don't really solve any problem for us. We are convinced we want it because we have been bombarded by images and videos telling us we want it. But think about it this way: if you had never seen the advertisement, would you have really sat at home wishing that the product existed? Probably not. This is a clear sign of a manufactured desire.

5. Compare down instead of up

When we start comparing our lives to people around us, we lose contentment, joy, and happiness. We begin focusing all our attention on eliminating this difference. That's because we tend to compare upward, only looking at people who have more than us. We must break the consumerism trap by taking notice of those who have less than us. This will help us remain joyful and grateful for what we currently have.

6. Consider the full cost of what you buy

When we purchase items, we tend to only look at the sticker price. But the number on the tag is not the full cost. What we buy always costs us extra energy, time, and focus. This also includes fixing, maintaining, organizing, cleaning, removing and replacing. Make a habit of considering these expenses before making a purchase. You'll find yourself making wiser and more confident decisions when it comes to money.

7. Turn off the TV

Corporations spend a huge amount of money on advertising because they know they can make consumers buy their products or services this way. Television is an industry built on the assumption that you can be persuaded to spend money on nearly anything. No one is immune and even if you don't realize it, TV has likely convinced you to buy something you normally wouldn't have. When you reduce the amount of time you spend watching TV, you are less likely to be persuaded to buy items you don't need.

8. Make gratitude a part of your life

Gratitude helps us to respond positively to our life circumstances and change our attitude during times of stress. Make it part of your life during the hardships, as well as periods of abundance. Start focusing on the blessings and not just your troubles. Studies have shown that gratitude practices increase our sense of happiness.

9. Practice generosity

Giving helps us to recognize how much we are blessed with and what else we have to offer. It allows us to find fulfillment and purpose in assisting others. When we act generously, we take on a mindset of abundance, and this can assist us in embracing minimalism. When we give to others, we begin to believe subconsciously that we have a lot more to spare.

It's worth noting that generosity leads us to contentment, and not the other way around. We should not wait to be content before acting generously.

10. Renew your commitment daily

Everywhere we go, we are flooded with advertisements. At times, it can almost feel overwhelming. We must continue to reject these consumerist ideologies and remain strong in the face of destructive excess. For total freedom, we must cultivate self-awareness and recommit ourselves to our goals every day. The best part is, the more we continue to commit ourselves, the easier it becomes. Soon this commitment to a better life becomes your new norm.

Quick Start Action Steps to free yourself from Compulsive Spending once and for all

At some point or another, we've all been caught up in excessive spending and its destructive cycle. Despite our best intentions, sometimes it can be hard to stop impulse purchases. And as soon as we start spending impulsively, it can be challenging to keep our finances on track. Every purchase is on the spur of the moment, and our actions are no longer conscious.

Although not formally recognized by medical research, compulsive spending is a serious issue, and it has been on the rise for the past few years. Your spending becomes compulsive when it's out of control, excessive and results in legal, social, or financial problems. But even if your consequences aren't as extreme, compulsive spending could still be a major issue you need to quit. Do you frequently make purchases that you can't really afford, yet you make them anyway? That is a problem, my friend.

Some people view spending as a confidence booster, as they think that buying new things makes them seem more glamorous and prosperous than they are. And of course, the public is inundated by billboards, print ads, commercials, and other advertisements to entice anyone with a compulsive spending habit. You think this way because big corporations want you to think this way.

To prevent needless purchases, you should know what you are shopping for and stay focused on exactly what it is you've set out to do. This is a sure way to safeguard against overspending.

If your finances are getting out of hand, you can regain some control with this step-by-step plan. Remember, money doesn't have to slip through your fingers!

1. Get to the root of the problem

Compulsive spenders accumulate a lot of stuff, but that's not the root of the problem. You must consider what you are really buying. Above all, compulsive spending is a response to an emotional problem. We feel some level of unrest or emptiness, and somehow, we have become convinced that a new purchase is the solution.

A person might be dealing with anxiety, depression, anger, or grief. These emotions can trigger spending, which may result in shame, fear, guilt, feelings of inadequacy, doubt, and many others.

You should identify your triggers and attempt to get them under control. It is recommended to seek professional therapy or support groups to help you manage your spending problem.

You should also consider talking to a friend, and sometimes they can be great therapists.

2. Pay in cash

People tend to spend more when they are paying with debit cards and credit cards. It's no wonder why. Charging bills to a piece of plastic can make you feel disconnected from money. It's easier to ignore what the cost means for your financial situation, and this can easily result in overspending.

Spending feels real when you take dollars out from your wallet. Start setting aside a portion of your income expressly for bills and withdrawing the rest in cash.

Chances are that you will not go on a compulsive spending binge since you can understand more acutely that you have a limited amount of money.

3. Give your purchases a score

Give every item you purchase a score based on how necessary it is to you. The more necessary it is, the higher the score. When you look back at your purchases, you'll see how much you can save by removing the unnecessary purchases. By eliminating low-scoring items, you'll be surprised by how much you can save.

Without scoring the items you buy, it can be difficult to know which purchases matter to you the most. Sooner or later you'll run low on money, with an excess of low-scoring items and possibly a lack of the high-scoring things you truly need.

When it comes to scoring items, you must be honest with yourself. Don't give something a higher score just because you really want it. Really consider how necessary it is. Can something else you own perform the same function? Will the quality of your life really suffer without it?

4. Wait at least 20 minutes before buying anything

When you spot an object you want to buy, your body takes over your mind and it can be difficult to think rationally. To avoid the urge to spend, try waiting for at least 20 minutes before making a purchase. Tell yourself that you can only make the purchase the item if you still feel it's necessary once you've walked away from it. After that time, you may realize you don't really want the item and resist the spending urge. When we are no longer faced with the item in question, it's easier for us to say no.

5. Find social connections

Compulsive spenders waste their money on material goods because they are trying to fill the need for human connection with shopping. The truth is, you can never have enough of the things you don't need. That's why you should learn to fill your life with activities and social connections instead. These activities can involve clubs, learning a new skill, charity groups, or sports.

Many people see shopping as the center of their social life, but it does not have to be this way. When you fill your life with new, meaningful experiences, there will be changes in how you spend and improved satisfaction overall.

6. Pay attention to your spending patterns

You need to know where your money is going. Track how you spend for a month and look for a trend. You might be surprised by the amount of money you lose on insignificant activities like lunch out or frequent coffees.

Take note of your necessary expenses and list them as your priorities. These include:

- Shelter and utilities
- Food
- Transportation
- Basic clothing

All this said, your necessities are no reason to splurge. You don't have to buy new clothes every week or go out to dinner every night. Check your monthly expenses so that you can find ways to trim the spending. Do you need that fancy satellite dish when you can stream your favorite shows on the internet? What about the $40 gym membership you haven't used in five months? Questions like this will help you stay on the path to healthy spending.

7. Spend money with a purpose

After putting together a monthly budget, create a spending plan to go along with it.

If you need concert tickets or new clothes, ensure that you add them to their budget categories after prioritizing your necessities.

You only need to withdraw the cash you need and sort it into labeled envelopes. For instance, if you choose to allocate $200 every month for groceries, set aside $100 after you receive the first paycheck and have it in a groceries envelope. Add the remaining amount when you get the second paycheck.

If your line of work has an unpredictable cash flow, consider creating a budget for irregular income.

You can use a free budgeting app to create your budget in no time. It will help you plan, monitor your debt, track your spending and monitor your saving process.

8. Shop with a goal

We've all bought things that we didn't plan. You go to the supermarket and all you need is toothpaste and shampoo, but as soon as you walk through the door, you end up filling your basket with stuff you'll probably only use once. A short trip to the store can become expensive when you're a compulsive spender.

No one plans to get sidetracked when they're shopping, but if you often find yourself spending needless amounts of money, consider planning your trip beforehand. As long as you stick to your plan, you won't have to worry about overspending.

9. Don't spend money on eating out

Changing your spending habits on food is an efficient way to cut down expenses. Many don't realize it, but dining out can get expensive very fast. If you spend $20 on lunch four times a week, it will cost you $80 per week and $320 per month.

Instead of eating out every day, make a meal plan for one week and buy the required groceries at the store. Make sure to bring a list so you only purchase what you intend to use for your home-cooked meals.

Lunchtime offers a perfect opportunity to cut back. Consider bringing lunch to work every day. Make it simple. Prepare meals on Sundays or take about twenty minutes every night to prepare a sandwich.

This doesn't mean you shouldn't treat yourself, it just means you need to stick to your budget. After all, you can still make delicious and cost-effective homemade meals.

10. Resist sales

We all love a good deal. Retailers understand this well and they know how flashy sales are irresistible to their customers. Sometimes a big sale can even get people to purchase items they don't really want; they just can't resist the deal, no matter how useless what they're buying is.

If you've ever bought something you didn't mean to buy just because it's 30% off, it means you paid 70% more than you intended. That's not saving money at all; you're still spending. It is essential that you start to practice self-discipline when you see a sale at the store.

Remind yourself that keeping all your money is far better than saving 30%.

11. Challenge yourself to achieve new goals

Strengthen your willpower by giving yourself new challenges. For example, try only to purchase your necessities for a month. You'll be surprised by how little you need.

This will also give you a chance to identify what you don't really need. Do you like paying for your monthly gym membership because it helps you stay active? Then keep it. Do you like going to a chiropractor because it keeps your back in good shape? Keep going. If it fits into the budget and is good for you, then keep enjoying it.

Chapter 2 - Start Saving Money

Do you ever wonder where that money goes? Do you earn a lot of money but still live paycheck to paycheck? Do you sometimes look at your savings and feel like you could do better?

If the answer to any of these questions is 'yes,' then you are not alone. You'd be surprised by the number high-income individuals who can't seem to save a penny. They spend with the mindset that there's lots of money to spare. Funnily enough, they end up having none of it to spare. It doesn't matter how much money you have; if you never spend responsibly, your bank balances will be much lower than they should be.

Most people who live paycheck to paycheck blame their finance issues on lifestyle purchases such as entertainment and dining. Most claim their lack of discipline continues to prevent them from achieving their goals. Their money is lost on things that could be avoided with a little extra effort and creativity.

If you want to achieve your financial goals, you must learn more about your spending habits, create foolproof plans to save money, and cultivate self-discipline in the face of temptation. How do you achieve all this? Let's discuss them individually.

Figure out where the heck all your money goes every month

It's good to have a budget, but if you aren't tracking your expenses, you'll lose track of this budget easily, defeating its entire purpose. You'll run the risk of setting unrealistic goals that you never meet. It is only when you discover where your money is going that you have a good idea of what to cut down. Many people are surprised at what they spend the most money on. You may think it's too many subscription services, but what if it's actually the $5 latte you have five days of the week?

This is the cycle that most people fall into. If you want to make a change, tracking your spending is a must. Here is how it works:

Steps to track your expenses

1. Create a budget

You need a budget to track your expenses. Without one, it would be a difficult challenge to work out what the biggest drain on your money is. A budget shows your expected income and all expenses by category.

A budget doesn't control you; you adjust it as you please. It serves as a guide to ensure your money does what you tell it to do.

There are three steps to creating a budget:

- Write down your monthly income.
- Write down your monthly expenses.

a) Start with shelter, food, transportation, and clothing.

b) When the necessities are covered, list other expenses like eating out, TV streaming services, savings, gym memberships, etc.

- Ensure that your income minus expenses comes to zero.

2. Record your expenses

Keep a record of your expenses every day. In a small notepad or your phone's Notes app, jot down everything you spend money on, from your morning cup of coffee to that new pair of shoes. If you fail to keep up with what you spend, you'll feel like you're in a fantasy land where money never runs out. This would be great – except it isn't the real world. Money does run out, and when it does, those consequences can hit you hard.

3. Watch those numbers

Make sure that when you note down your expenses, you track how much is left in the category. This way you'll have a better idea of when the cost of something is too high.

If you are married, talk with your partner and ensure you both record all spending that takes place. Make sure to check in with each other before spending. This practice is excellent for igniting great communication and accountability.

Budgets are blown when you fail to track and watch how you spend.

4 Ways to track your expenses

As we've demonstrated, tracking your expenses is a very important practice. There are also many ways that you can do it. Each method comes with its own advantages and disadvantages. Finding which one suits you best can shape your entire experience of budgeting, determining whether this habit becomes a permanent part of your lifestyle or not. Feel free to try each one out to see for yourself.

1. Paper and pencil

Old-school methods are still extremely helpful. Many people prefer to keep track of their budget on paper. The benefit of physical writing is that it requires an active brain. An active brain will remember more clearly what was written down, so all numbers in the budget are always carefully considered. Using ink and paper also means you can use gel pens and other coloring tools that can make your expense-tracking more fun. The bright colors might even make your task feel less daunting.

The downside to this method is that most of us don't keep paper copies anymore. When you receive a receipt, you must hold onto it until the budget is updated. It's also more difficult to make amendments if you discover you recorded something inaccurately.

You'll likely find yourself misplacing receipts. Sometimes you simply forget to ask for one. Sometimes certain purchases don't get written down. Any of these issues can lead to problematic tracking. And if you lose your expense-tracking sheet, it'll be a big drag to start all over.

2. The envelope system

This method involves paying cash in person. You can create special allocations for utilities, mortgage, and retirement. You can make a debit card payment online or send checks for other utilities. But the expenses you pay in person should only be in cash.

At the beginning of the month, place cash in envelopes labeled with the budget lines. Eating out, entertainment and groceries are the three perfect examples. Remember to carry the groceries envelope with you whenever you go to a grocery store. When the envelope is empty, that's when you stop spending. Using this method, your money will essentially be tracking itself.

Well, the truth is, paying in cash can sometimes be inconvenient. Who likes keeping up with coins or counting out bills? Who wants to go inside a gas station to prepay at the register? Plus, with the recent increase in e-commerce, cash payment options aren't always available. However, this is a great way to track your expenses. That's because watching the envelope become empty will inspire a new level of responsibility.

3. Computer spreadsheets

Many people have gone digital and most of them are spreadsheet fanatics. They love discussing spreadsheet perks, and if you don't know what they're talking about, you probably couldn't care less. The reality is, however, that spreadsheets offer plenty of benefits. This includes the ability to customize your budget, use a plethora of templates, and last but not least, all the math is done for you.

Minimalist Budget

Unfortunately, spreadsheet enthusiasts don't always find a fellow spreadsheet enthusiast. It's likely that only one partner will want to use it. Couples should communicate openly about their preferences. You shouldn't let spreadsheets come between a happy marriage.

Another problem with spreadsheets is getting your computer to keep up with the spending. If you fail to log these expenses daily, your budget won't be a budget at all, just a spreadsheet with good but empty intentions. We all have good intentions in the beginning, but they don't accomplish financial goals on their own.

It's probable that you spend a decent amount of time on the computer, so perhaps spreadsheets will work for you. But do you know what else will always be at your side? Your phone. That brings us to the next and best option for tracking expenses.

4. Budgeting apps

There are a lot of free budgeting apps that will create a budget in just a few minutes. You can easily log in to your phone and enter your expenses the moment they occur. You won't have to go about your day, risking forgetfulness about your budget updates.

That's how convenient a budgeting app is. Some of these apps let you customize your templates to meet your saving and spending goals. The best part is you can sync your budget with your partner's devices and be in constant commerce communication.

No matter the method you choose, make tracking your expenses a habit if you want to achieve your financial goals. If you fail to track your money, you will always be wondering where your money went. But with the right tools and self-discipline, you can achieve financial victories.

11 simple ways to instantly start saving money

You work hard to earn your money, so it should also work hard for you. Intentionality is the key to making your money go the extra mile. Being intentional is how you'll start saving more and spending less each month. When we are intentional with our money, we know where each penny is going. Every time we swipe our credit card or pull a bill out of our wallet, we are aware of why we are doing it and it is not done out of impulse. This, in turn, keeps more of our money in our account.

There are a lot of ways to save money. Where do you start? Start easy. Start quick. Start here. These are 8 simple tips to help you save money every day, week, month, or year. Here they are:

1. Get cheaper alternatives

If you want to save money, reduce what you spend. There are ways to do this so you still get what you need, but at a much smaller cost. For instance, if you love shopping, consider taking advantage of coupons. You can save money by using cash back or coupons from money-saving apps. Many will let you know about the best prices available on certain items. You can download these apps from your favorite stores and there are a lot of ways you can save money by using them. You can check out sales, nab coupons and join reward programs. Just make sure to resist the temptation to shop online.

You can also look for other alternatives by getting used items. Instead of getting a new item, you can get something used but still in good condition at a lower price. When it comes to buying used items, your discretion is required. Some things cannot be bought used like tires and a toothbrush. But if you're looking for a car, books, video games, tools, or pets, then you can save a lot of money by buying gently used items.

If you love exercising and currently pay for a gym membership, consider other means like finding workout videos online. Some people need the human interaction we get at the gym, while others prefer to lose weight without a membership, special class fees, and a personal trainer. If you want to burn calories without incurring huge monthly expenses, consider exercise-streaming services and

YouTube videos. Many fitness gurus have realized that we need non-DVD options we can use at home, and they are creating high-quality content that we can enjoy anytime from the comfort of our home.

Aside from these options, you can also consider brewing your own coffee instead of buying it, and you can cook at home instead of paying for meals at a restaurant. If you spend about $5 per day on your favorite barista blend, it would cost you $35 per week and about $150 per month. Instead of this, you can spend just $20 a month brewing your own and you'll save $130. You can put these savings towards greater things like your dream vacation, retirement, a sinking fund, or whatever your goals are financially.

Instead of paying for an expensive form of entertainment, consider free options. How about e-books, audiobooks, physical books, movies, performances or presentations? Where do you get all of this? At a local library, of course. Get a library card now!

Save money and still have fun.

2. Eliminate the things you don't need

You can save a significant amount of money by eliminating goods, subscriptions, and other services that you don't really need. Do you really need different music and TV streaming services? How many subscription magazines or boxes show up in your mail each month? I am not saying you should avoid these services, but if you haven't thought about them in a while, chances are that you're subscribed to services you don't use, read or watch any more. If you want to save some money, cut out any monthly subscriptions that you no longer have use for.

You can also make further eliminations by evaluating your TV choices. If you pay high cable package prices and only end up watching a few channels, then you are not alone. A lot of people are realizing they can save a large amount of money and still watch the shows they want by choosing other options.

Consider Vimeo, YouTube, Amazon Prime Video, Netflix, or Hulu. Consider watching recently aired episodes online. Or try using that library card.

You don't have to return to medieval times where the only entertainment was watching a joust. You just have to trade that cable bill for a cheaper but equally awesome option.

3. Eliminate expense-increasing practices

Don't wait for expenses to accumulate before making a change. For starters, consider making more energy-efficient life choices. Some of these might require big initial investments, but they pay off in the end. To save on home expenses, turn off the lights when you leave home, buy energy-saving light bulbs, take quick showers and purchase a programmable thermostat.

To save on transportation costs, use public transportation, carpool, or consider biking. These green options will do wonders for your savings as well as the planet.

If you're considering buying a video game console, think twice. Having a console only means you'll want to spend more money on games. This is an expensive purchase that will only lead to even more expensive purchases.

You should also avoid credit cards so you don't find yourself getting into debt. A great first step to getting ahead is to stop getting behind. That sounds logical, doesn't it? Credit cards are easy ways to fall behind. After all, this is how you accumulate debt in the first place. Debt gives us the illusion of ownership. It keeps out the sunshine of true ownership, however, as it's like a grey, hovering cloud of obligation.

Stop using credit cards, and you will start owning for real. Instead of making debt payments, how about make savings? Not only is this an empowering life change, but you'll thank yourself for it later.

Once you've gotten rid of credit cards, consider removing your debit card information from online shops. The quickest way to spend money these days is through the "one-click" feature. This is when websites store your payment information and make purchases far too easy with a single click of a button. When buying is so easy, overspending is extremely likely. Take your time to retrieve your wallet, pull out your debit card, and do the tedious job of entering all the numbers. As you are going about this arduous process, consider whether this purchase is worth it. Imagine yourself making that transaction and how it will affect your budget. If you still think it's a good idea after thinking it through, then go ahead as you intended.

You can also reduce your future expenses by performing a maintenance check on household objects, such as appliances and cars. Most of these things can be very expensive when replacing or repairing, and a monthly routine check can save you from future financial headaches. Have your car cleaned, checked, and fill the air in the tires when needed. Clean out home vents and remember to check any wear and tear on appliances.

Sometimes a simple bolt, washer, screw replacement, or cleaning can keep it running efficiently.

Before you shop, you should always give it some thought. You don't want to incur huge expenses for something you won't use. Always sleep on a huge decision before taking the plunge. Perhaps even, take a few days. Take the time to check on prices, compare their advantages and disadvantages, and perform desire measuring.

What is desire measuring, you ask? You think you want that trendy, weather-proof laptop case the moment you see it. But does the desire reduce with time? Impulse buying can be expensive. Practice patience to avoid running your wallet dry.

4. Spend creatively

If you want to save money and still get what you want, consider creative ways to find a balance. For instance, a date doesn't have to be expensive to be exciting. There's this pervasive myth that spending a lot of money on a date will guarantee you the love of your life. The truth is, money has nothing to do with it. You can fall in love and have fun while still adhering to minimalist practices.

Consider filling a picnic basket with apples, popcorn, chocolate, and an assortment of cheeses. You can also bring home Chinese takeout and eat while you watch your favorite show. Or how about hanging out at the park? There are many ways to enjoy a date without making your bank account suffer. And if your date can't enjoy the simple things in life, is this really someone you want to see permanently? You might find that minimalism opens your eyes to all the shallow and superficial people in your life. Good riddance!

Consider engaging in more outdoor activities for fun. These activities can offer great entertainment and most don't require a lot of money. There are plenty of things about nature to find fascinating. Consider biking, hiking, spiking, backpacking, kayaking, stargazing, corn-mazing, or curtain-raising. Get out, have fun and save up.

5. Sell what you don't need

Clutter can give us the illusion of completion, but it is the furthest thing from it. Clutter is made up of stuff that nobody really needs. It can be a drain on your energy, overwhelming corners, closets, and drawers all over your house. Having clutter in your vicinity can cloud your sense of clarity. Catching sight of overflowing cupboards may make you feel like your mind, too, is overflowing.

You can cash in by selling the items that you don't need. Post about them online, take them to a consignment shop, or have an old-fashioned garage sale. There are also numerous apps that provide an inviting and fun platform for others to purchase second-hand items. For clothes, try using Vinted, and for all used books, why not hop on Amazon?

Reduce the number of possessions you don't need, create a calmer home environment, and make cash while you do it.

6. Get excited about borrowing instead of buying

Chances are, if there's something you really need temporarily, someone you know already owns it. Perhaps you're going to a black-tie event and you don't own the right kind of blazer. Perhaps you're looking for a new book to read. Before heading to the store and pulling out your wallet, why not ask your friends if they have something you can borrow? There's a high likelihood they have something you can use. This means you have exactly what you need, and you get to save yourself some money and some extra clutter. Borrowing can be exciting! You can make anyone's stuff your stuff temporarily, and you don't need to pay for it. Just make sure to give it back in good condition as soon as you no longer need it.

7. Take advantage of offers and promos

Businesses provide all kinds of offers to their customers. Try to take advantage of these offers and save money this way. For example, when you're at a restaurant, take advantage of the happy hour specials. These days it extends to meals and not just drinks.

You should also consider eating apps. Subscribe for newsletters from your favorite restaurants, and they'll send you promos and coupons. By eating at a lower cost, you'll save money. And consider unsubscribing from stores or restaurants that tend to make you overspend. This requires some awareness of your spending patterns.

Check the bottom of your receipts as certain restaurants may offer discounts if you take a survey. You can make big savings in exchange for some of your time.

You can also hit up weekly ads and BOGOs. Stores with BOGO offers are practically begging you to save some money. Follow this money-saving move: create a meal plan based on your store's sales. Consider stocking up the freezer and pantry for the future. Keep in mind what you bought when making meal plans, for the future.

8. Make a shopping list and stick to your budget

Begin by planning your meals – decide on what you will eat at dinner, lunch, and breakfast for a whole week. Then make a list of the individual groceries you'll need to make those meals happen, keeping in mind your budget. You may find that purchasing separate ingredients is more cost-effective than buying many premade meals. Regardless of your preference, always stick to the list you make. This will keep you from overspending and forgetting items in your grocery budget.

9. Always ask for fees to be waived

When signing up for something, there may be some fees that are involved, and we always end up paying it. You'd be surprised how accommodating certain companies can be when you ask for a fee waiver.

In a recent survey conducted, it was found that over half of responders were successful in getting a bank or other financial institution to waive a fee. The most common fees to get waived are overdraft fees, followed closely by late payment fees.

Doing that won't make you rich, but some extra cash from waived fees can still be helpful. Not all companies will agree to this, but it never hurts to ask. Just make sure to explain your situation honestly and you find yourself being met with a compassionate fee waiver.

10. Skip the cheap stuff for lasting purchases

Buying cheaper items may save you money in the short-term, but if you want long-term savings, avoid them. It's no secret that cheap stuff tends to be lower in quality. What does that mean? Fragile items that are a lot more breakable. Once it breaks, you'll have to replace it. And that means spending yet more money on a replacement. If you continue to buy something cheap, this cycle will only continue. Eventually, you'll find you've spent a large amount of money on a dozen low-quality things, when you could have spent less money on one high-quality thing. To improve your savings, only purchase items that you know will last.

11. Say a permanent 'no' to one-time-use items

If you're only going to use the item once, do not purchase it. This only applies to non-food items, of course. Were you invited to a 20's themed party but you don't have any 20's themed clothes? You're probably thinking you should head to the store right now to buy a whole new outfit, but this is the opposite of what you should do. This will result not only in clutter, but needless money-spending. Do not purchase items you don't see yourself using for the rest of your life. A better option? Borrow the clothes. They'll be free if you borrow them from someone you know, or at the very least, cheaper than something brand new if you find a store that loans what you need.

How to develop self-discipline to stop yourself from overspending

We start off every month with the intention to save money, by only buying the things we need, staying away from sales displays, and watching our spending closely. Despite our best efforts, we may still find ourselves spending more than we wanted. Sometimes it can even feel like money just slips through our fingers.

Don't beat yourself up, this happens to most of us. There are many reasons why we might overspend. Sometimes it's because we aren't aware of our spending habits. Or because we've estimated our income, debt payments, and expenses incorrectly. This leads to the numbers in our bank account dipping lower than they should. Whatever the reason, if you're ready to take control of your money, here are some useful tips you can apply to develop the personal discipline to stop overspending.

1. Know your spending triggers

To develop self-discipline around spending, you must identify the physical and emotional triggers that make you spend. Once you're aware of these triggers, you can begin to eliminate the opportunity and temptation to overspend. Keep in mind:

Time of the day – Do you have more energy during certain periods of the day? If that's the case, shop only when you have more energy. This way, you'll make wise spending choices. After all, we can think much clearly when we're less pressured and more relaxed.

Environment – Are there certain environments that make you feel like spending? Shopping malls, craft fairs, home shows, and holidays are some examples of occasions on which you're likely to spend impulsively.

You can fight the temptation by taking less money with you or avoiding such environments.

Additionally, if you have a favorite store and sometimes you find yourself wandering through the aisles looking for amazing deals, try to limit the number of times you go there. If you simply can't limit your visits, keep your credit card and money safe from yourself, or ask someone you trust to do it for you.

Mood – Different emotional states and moods can change our energetic resources, making us overspend. For instance, if we're anxious, stressed or upset, we may take retail therapy a little too far.

Instead of going to the mall, try hitting up the park or the gym. Exercise and fresh air will do wonders for improving your mood.

It is important to identify the moods that result in your bad shopping habits. Once these moods strike, go somewhere your wallet doesn't need to be involved.

Peer pressure – Do you spend more money than you should when you're hanging out with friends? Even our best friends with the best intentions can be a bad influence, especially if they also have bad spending habits. When you can't afford to eat out, shop, or go on holiday, it's okay to decline their invitations. Feel free to be honest since they are likely to understand.

Or instead, suggest plans that won't make you spend more money. You can meet for coffee instead of brunch, explore new hiking trails instead of going to a concert or have a potluck dinner at home instead of eating at a restaurant.

You may not be having fancy dinners or expensive vacations, but you can still enjoy a great social life. On a minimalist budget, your social connections will not be sacrificed.

If you let your friends know you're trying to spend less, they can even help you on your journey, and some of them may want to follow in your footsteps. The most important thing is finding friends who will support you in achieving your financial goals.

Lifestyle – If you're used to a certain lifestyle, it can be difficult to give it up when faced with financial hardship. But if the overspending continues, you'll only end up in worse shape.

Your upbringing may have influenced your lifestyle choices. If you were brought up in a household where money was tight, you might feel the urge to spend more to compensate for the things you didn't get. Conversely, if you grew up in a family where money wasn't an issue, you'll want to maintain the lifestyle you grew up with. This can be financially detrimental if your source of money isn't the same as it used to be.

The easiest way to live within your means is to find cheaper alternatives. You may have to sacrifice a little bit of comfort, but it's better than losing a lot of comfort when your bank account gets in the red. It can be hard to give up certain luxuries, but no one's quality of life is compromised by this. Most luxury items are excessive, and you'll find that 'above average' brands, as opposed to high-end brands, are still extremely satisfying.

2. List your priorities

You need to categorize your monthly expenses into three main categories: wants, needs, and nice-to-have. Include expenses like car payments, rent, groceries, and utilities in the needs category. Items like new clothes or unnecessary gadgets should go under the wants category. Premium cable channels and entertainment should be listed in the nice-to-have category.

You should establish your goals based on this list. Consider casting the goals in positive terms, and not as things you have to live without. If you always spend $5 each day on fast food lunches, try cutting back to two fast-food lunches per week. Consider bringing lunch from home for the other three days. The extra $15 can be put towards one of your other goals. This will help in debt reduction and still satisfy your fast food cravings. This self-discipline can easily turn into a positive, lasting habit.

3. Learn to budget money

Without a plan, you won't stop erratic spending. If we fail to learn how much we take home and how much we spend, we will keep buying what we think we can afford. You will only realize after a month that you've wasted money when your bank account is empty and there's no taking your bad decisions back. To avoid this, learn to budget your money.

Start by adding up all your sources of income and then all your fixed expenses like debt repayments, rent, car payment, etc. The fixed expenses are easier to budget.

When that is done, list your variable expenses like gas, groceries, and entertainment and allocate funds to each category based on how much you've spent in the past.

Seeing how much you spend on clothing, entertainment, and other wants can help you save on what you don't need.

Try testing your budget. Track your spending for a month and compare that to what you've allocated in your budget. Make all necessary changes to your budget in the next month.

4. Track your spending

The little purchases we make can add up to a huge amount. Without tracking them, your regrets will grow, too. Tracking expenses is the key to successful budgeting. It will keep you accountable for every dollar you spend. When you know where your money goes, it helps you make better choices in the future.

Many people start tracking bigger expenses, but it's crucial to pay attention to the smaller purchases as well. Those lunches out, morning lattes, lottery tickets, or magazine purchases can add up to more than you expect. In fact, you'll find that sometimes they can cost more than the bigger expenses, in the long run. This can affect your budget in significant ways.

5. Evaluate yourself honestly

Every month, compare your spending to what you intended to spend. It's a great time to hold yourself accountable. If you tend to overspend for certain categories, it's time to admit these are your problem areas. Stop making excuses for why you lost control and start reflecting on the real reason you've chosen to spend your money this way.

Minimalist Budget

You need to be honest with yourself since the only person who suffers from this lack of discipline is you. Hold yourself to higher standards and know when it's time to get serious with yourself. Whatever the reason for your overspending is, there is most certainly an alternative that both fulfills the same need and is kinder to your wallet. Get creative and think about what these alternatives could be.

6. Spend wisely

Set aside money every month to cover all your required bills and expenses. Whether you set aside money on your computer or physically, make sure this is a habit you get used to. Resist all temptations to spend money on things other than the expenses.

Pay as many or as much of your bills as you can. Paying more towards your credit card bill, for instance, will reduce your owed balance quickly and save money on interest.

You can buy a "want" every two months so you don't feel deprived.

Resist the urge to get a new purse or the latest tech gadget that's all the rage. Instead, put these items on your birthday wish list or for any other holiday you celebrate. You can also set up a money jar for that item, and put change from your purse or pocket into it every evening. If you used a coupon at a store, put the amount you saved into the jar. Try selling unused items online or at a garage sale, and put the money you earned in the savings jar.

You'll be surprised by how easy money adds up without taking anything away from your monthly bills.

7. Pay off expenses

Make it easy to resist impulsive buying. Consider only carrying the cash you have budgeted for. And perhaps allow yourself a low-interest credit card only for when you really need it. Make sure to only use this credit card when it is absolutely necessary. Even a low-interest credit card can cause you significant debt if it is not used wisely.

Use unexpected income – tax refunds, birthday gifts, annual bonuses – to pay off a high-interest credit card or loan. Remind yourself that putting extra money towards your needs lets you make inroads into main expenses and allows you to pay them off sooner.

8. Reward yourself

Reward yourself when you've achieved significant goals. For example, after you've paid off a huge bill or successfully maintained self-discipline for a long period of time.

After renting movies for a whole month, reward yourself with a show at your local theatre. If you've successfully refrained from eating out on the weekends, reward yourself with one dinner out every month. You've saved money and made progress towards more disciplined spending habits. This is something worth celebrating – just make sure the celebration is within budget!

9. Define your motivations

It's crucial to understand what achieving financial security means for you. It could mean having the freedom to do whatever you want. Or perhaps it's travel, spending more time with family, or more time to write a novel.

Here are other examples to consider:

- Retiring early
- Having more money for hobbies
- Starting a non-profit organization
- Quitting your job and for a passion that offers lower pay or less stability

Whatever your true motivation is, it's crucial that you identify it and keep it in mind when you feel the nudge of spending urges. Try to figure out how else financial self-discipline can assist you in getting there and what the smaller steps to that destination are. Your motivations may also change over time. Make sure you can adapt to these changes.

10. Ditch the credit cards

When going to the grocery store or the mall, take the amount you think will be enough and leave the credit card at home. Unless you're sure you can pay it off soon, you shouldn't take credit cards with you at all.

This way you'll avoid impulse spending and the risk of getting into any debt. It's easy to make yourself promises in the heat of a shopping spree. Promises such as, "I'll just be more sensible the next couple of weeks and I can easily pay this off." But the next week, you end up saying the same thing, with no change to your behaviour. Eliminate the possibility of this happening and leave that credit card at home.

Having credit card information saved onto your online shopping profile can make it easy to spend impulsively. All it takes you is a click, and you'll be just a few shoes richer and a lot of dollars poorer.

When you delete these credit card numbers, you make it slightly less convenient to purchase needless items.

11. Set short-term financial goals

Setting attainable, short-term money goals is a perfect way to remain motivated as you change your spending habits. These goals will constantly remind you of the reasons why you are cutting back on expenses. It's important to focus on short-term goals because long-term goals can seem daunting. It'll take a long time before you achieve a long-term goal (hence the word long-term!) and you may feel you're not making progress. Watching your short-term goals get ticked off will motivate you to keep going. Break up your long-term goals into small, achievable steps.

And, it's also crucial to set specific goals. A goal like 'reduce spending on eating out' isn't going to work well because it isn't specific. You need quantifiable goals like 'I will reduce how much I spend on eating out from $150 to $75 a month.' These goals will give you a target to aim for.

Some other short-term goals include:
- Saving 10% of all paychecks in a different account
- Sticking to a cash budget
- Bringing lunch to work for a whole month

Regardless of your goals, it's important you keep them simple, attainable and out in the open to remind yourself daily.

Chapter 3 - Budgeting Strategies and Financial Plans

Budgeting and saving don't work for many people and for obvious reasons. Even when you have a well-laid out plan, spending on nonessentials is far too easy and straying from our goal is a common occurrence.

The basic concept behind budgeting is simple, but it's in the execution where people fail. To save money, all you need to do is not spend it. I mean, how hard can that be? This is what most of us tell ourselves when we try to establish money habits, but something always makes us lose focus.

There are a lot of budgeting strategies. Different strategies work for different people. You won't find a single budgeting strategy that works for everyone. With the right planning, diligence, and perseverance, it's possible to create and maintain an effective budget.

Before implementing a budgeting or financial plan, you need to know your reason for doing so. If you don't, chances are you won't want to create a budget. And even if you do create a budget, you aren't likely to stick to it if you don't know why it exists in the first place. Perhaps you have been reckless with your spending and you want to stop impulse purchases immediately. Or maybe you're on a debt repayment plan. Or perhaps you are good with your money, but you aren't making great headway on your long-term goals. Whatever the reason, start defining why you want to create a budget. This will keep you focused.

You will also have to figure out your priorities. Budgeting isn't all about math and numbers. It's about living the best way you can by improving your relationship with money. It's about finding out what's important to you and then changing your spending habits to meet your goals and values.

If you have money goals, write them down. Concentrate on the top priorities. The most important thing when concentrating on priorities is honesty. If your priorities are dishonest and don't reflect your personal values, you will be conflicted when making crucial decisions. You'll find it hard to stay motivated and on task. Be yourself when it comes to budgeting.

You also have to monitor your outflow. It's important to do this before and after creating a budget. That's because it can be impossible to know how much to allocate towards certain items without knowing how much you spend in a month. There are many apps and services that allow you to separate spending into categories.

You might discover something that will surprise you. You could find that while you feel you don't make enough, you make more than enough to cover all your expenses and still save for an emergency. Knowing where you stand will help you figure out where you want to be. If you learn that you make enough to save every month, you might want to see where you can cut back to start saving on emergency funds.

Now that you know what it takes to implement a budgeting strategy, we can take a deeper look.

4 powerful budgeting strategies to align your spending with your money-saving goals

There are a lot of ways you can approach budgeting. Some are very simple, while others are more complex and detailed. No method is better than the other. You just have to find a method that fits with your goals and personality. It's vital that you examine each one to determine which method suits you. The most common ones are:

1. 50/30/20 budgeting rule

With this rule, you spend 50% of your pay on needs like debts, insurance, groceries, utilities, and housing. 30% will go towards the expenses of your personal lifestyle. We can also label these as 'wants.' These expenses are the most likely to blow your budget out of order, so it's the most important to keep under control. It encompasses the things that you can do without, but make you happy nonetheless.

The remaining 20% of your income goes towards savings. This could be saved for retirement, working towards goals, or putting money into an investment. Use these on saving for a car, dream vacation, your children's college fund, and a house.

So, if you earn $5,000 every month, $2,500 should go towards your needs. $1,500 can be spent for your wants, and the remainder should be saved.

Some needs are obvious, but figuring out if something is a want or a need can be challenging. For example, work clothes would be a need, while trendy clothes to go out in would be classified as wants. You might need a monthly subscription service to back up your digital files to the cloud, but a music streaming service would be a want.

It is vital to categorize your needs and wants accordingly to stay on track.

2. Zero-sum budget

In this budget strategy, every dollar you make is assigned a job. The amount of money you make minus your expenses should come to zero.

So, if your total income is $5,000 per month, find a place where that money will go. You should break up your budget into different categories. Consider car-related expenses, eating out, rent and utilities, personal items, groceries, debt, and insurance. If you've covered all your expenses and still have $500 left, you need to assign a task to those remaining dollars.

The value of this budgeting strategy is that it leaves nothing without a task. Every dollar is accounted for and used the way you want.

The best way you can approach a zero-sum budget is by writing it all down. Find out your anticipated income before the start of the month, then create a budget in which those dollars will go and make required adjustments as you progress.

3. Anti-budget

Contrary to what the name of this budget strategy suggests, it is still a spending plan of sorts. In this strategy, you won't have to worry about putting your expenses in specific categories. You pay as you go. The only catch is you must pay for your priorities first. You immediately pay all your necessary bills, such as rent and utilities, put a small portion in your retirement fund, and another portion in your savings account (we advise saving at least 20% of your income) and *voila!* You can spend the rest however you like. No tedious writing or flicking aimlessly through your bank statements.

Minimalist Budget

This budgeting strategy is perfect for those who want to budget but have trouble starting. This requires consistency and an understanding of your priorities.

Define your priorities and make needs a priority before considering wants. Spend what you have on the necessities, then when all is paid, you can spend the rest on wants.

4. Money flow budgeting

With this budgeting strategy, some trial and error is required.

When you have figured out how much you need each month to pay for all expenses, you can create a money flow. How does that work? The best way is to figure out what all your recurring expenses are and set up auto-pay for each of them. This includes fixed necessities such as utilities and rent. You will be paying off these expenses directly from your checking account. After money flows in on payday, your bills are paid as soon as they are due. You won't have to touch anything.

This budgeting strategy is best for those who want to forget about when bills are due. You must be comfortable with bill pay automation and of course, you must make the effort to arrange for this in the beginning.

When all the fixed expenses have been paid, take the rest of your income and make a budget. That means that you'll only monitor discretional and variable spending. This includes gas for the car, entertainment, groceries, etc. If you feel like it, you can also move this money into a separate debit card or bank account.

Better yet, if self-monitoring works well for you, you can use a credit card to manage variable expenses. Just make sure to pay the balance in full as the month ends.

You will still have to review your spending regularly and make changes if you feel you aren't making progress. The ideal outcome from this strategy is you'll do less monthly work, and be aware of everything that happens with your money. Even if most of the work is automated, it doesn't mean you get to stop paying attention.

One of these strategies will be suitable for you; you just need to discover which one it is. The approach you choose depends on how you work best, how much work you can put, and the details you want to insert into your budget. The most important thing is that you prioritize making a budget.

Making sure that budget strategy implementation is successful

1. Use your budget

A budget is useless if you don't use it. When you have identified a budget strategy that feels right for you, consider trying it out. Personal finance involves a lot of trial and error. Don't worry if you test out a strategy and it doesn't work. Just try another one instead. Your ideal budgeting strategy will depend on your lifestyle and personal taste. It's important that you find the one that works for you.

2. Update your budget regularly

You will always find room for improvement. Make it a habit to review and change your budget at regular intervals to get maximized benefits from your money. Budgeting takes time. Make a budget, live with it, and over time you'll notice what doesn't work, and you can adjust accordingly. Don't be discouraged if your lifestyle doesn't seem to fit the budget you've created. Feel free to tweak certain aspects until it works for you.

There are no rules you can apply to improve your budget. Personal satisfaction should be your guideline. Are you satisfied with your monthly money management? Are you saving what you need? Are you able to adhere to the rules you've assigned? If you aren't, consider why.

3. Use existing habits to create new ones

Consider an established habit and use it to implement a new one. For example, let's say you always drink coffee every morning before heading to work. If you want to be better at checking how much money is left in your budget, connect these two habits in your daily routine. After drinking a cup of coffee, consider using a money app, or logging in to your bank account to check the balance. Checking your balance every time you drink a cup of coffee makes it easy to remember. As soon as you sit down with that cup of coffee, muscle memory will immediately have you examining your finances. Once this becomes part of your daily routine, you'll have total awareness of your financial standing at all times, making it less likely for you to make decisions that negatively impact it. The new habit of checking on your budget is easy to implement when you link it to a habit you are used to. Try it!

15 Easy steps to come up with a financial plan that lets you save more and earn more

A financial plan is a road map to guide you to a better future. It extends beyond just investing and budgeting. A good financial plan will help you navigate major financial milestones.

A financial plan acts as a set of principles or rules by which you live. The rules of your financial plan should help you in the grand scheme of your life. You need to have a flexible financial plan that allows you to adjust course when life gets tough. The core principles might stay the same, but finances can quickly change when you get married, buy a house, have kids, suffer from a disability or illness, get divorced, gear up for retirement or move across the country. A financial plan should act as a compass to get you back on track.

Your financial advisor might help you set up a plan, but most advisors are focused on product sales such as insurance, investments, and mortgages. Chances are they won't ask where you want to be in the next five years. Also, they might not truly understand your long and short-term money needs.

A better option is to work with a fee-only money advisor. They'll look at your financial health and come up with a plan to help you achieve your goals. The only problem is there are few fee-only advisors and a comprehensive plan might set you back thousands of dollars.

Another good idea is to create a basic financial plan. This process will make you think about money in ways you've never considered before.

Here are simple steps to help you create your financial plan:

1. **Identify your goals**

You must decide precisely what you want from your finances and which strategies will help you accomplish this.

Minimalist Budget

Do you have children that are expected to attend college someday? If so, you need to save money to make that happen.

At what age do you intend to retire? Knowing this will help you figure out your goal and just how much time you have to achieve it.

Do you want to get out of debt completely? If so, add up all your debt, and determine how much you have to pay towards it each month to clear it in a particular amount of time.

You can also work with a financial planner to target the most realistic and worthwhile goals. Sometimes planners will tell their clients what they want to hear, but a good planner will tell clients what they need to hear.

Also, remember that paying your financial planner is a huge waste if you don't use their advice. It would be like going to a doctor and then failing to take the prescribed medication.

When you have established your goals, identify a solid plan.

2. Setting up a budget

All financial planning requires you to spend less money than you make. Whether your goal is to retire early or pay off your mortgage, you need extra money to make such a goal a reality. That's why you need a budget. You will find that many people skip this step, which is why they never achieve any meaningful financial goals.

A lot of people think that budgets add stress, but most of the time, it does the opposite.

3. Cutting expenses

Identify the necessary expenses in your budget. These are what you must pay no matter what. Then identify the expenses that are important but that you could live without. These are necessary, can be cut to some degree.

Identify the discretionary expenses. These may be desirable, but they are not necessary. You can completely eliminate these expenses without affecting your survival.

When you have all your expenses in proper categories, it's time to make reductions. Reduce important expenses and eliminate some discretionary expenses.

4. Eliminate debt

It doesn't make sense to invest and save money when you are paying a lot of interest on the debt you owe.

Getting out of debt requires discipline, but it's possible. If you're in a lot of debt, you must drastically cut spending and increase earnings to pay it off quickly. Include all your debt except the first mortgage on your home.

When you are out of debt, set up systems that will prevent you from going back into debt. This includes setting aside money for big purchases and carrying the right health insurance so you don't take on sudden medical debt.

5. Build an emergency fund

When you are out of debt, consider building an emergency fund that can cater to your expenses for six months. This cushion will allow you to leave your investments alone during hard times. This should only be used for real emergencies like job loss, to protect retirement savings and investments.

If you must dip into the emergency fund, focus on returning the money as soon as possible. If you have an unstable job, you should consider saving up to cater for expenses for one year should an emergency arise.

If you are creating a financial plan while still paying off debt, set up a smaller emergency fund of about $1,500 or a month's income to help you cover unexpected expenses. This will ensure you get out of debt without adding more debt.

6. Determine your net worth

Figure out where you are before thinking about where you want to be. Create a net worth statement to get an idea of your financial situation.

Sum up all your assets and subtract the liabilities. What remains is your net worth. Play around with reduced versions of your current expenses. Seeing the final amount just might motivate you to make cut those expenses for real!

7. Check your cash flow

If you want a strong financial plan, you should understand how much you save and spend. You can use an app or spreadsheet to track the money that comes in from interest, wages, and government benefits, and the money that goes out for debt payments, rent, and utility bills.

Fill your monthly expenses in a column and the annual expenses in a different column. Add up the expenses in both columns and then subtract them from the total net income on a yearly and monthly basis. You will get your cash flow surplus or deficit.

Tracking your cash flow will give you a sense of confidence and control which makes it easier to implement financial changes.

8. Match your goals to your spending

Since you have identified your goals and determined the cash flow, it's time to compare your goals to your spending. How well do your spending habits mesh with your goals? If you continue with the spending habits that you have now, will you ever reach your goals? If so, how long will it take?

If there's a cash flow deficit, it means you won't meet your goal, so you'll have to reduce certain expenses to ensure there's money left over. If there is a cash surplus, then you can begin allocating money to meet your goals. Make sure that you put your priorities before your non-essentials.

9. Review your insurance coverage

Many employer plans provide minimal life insurance coverage. Basic calculations will help you determine if it covers enough. You should ensure that your life insurance is enough to pay off the debts you owe. Also, it should cover ten times your income when you have kids below the age of 10, and five times your income if you have kids above 10.

10. Reduce taxes

Most families have a straightforward tax plan and chances are that you already take advantage of the best tax shelters when owning a home or when you contribute to your TFSA, RRSP, and RESP.

But if you are self-employed and rely on rental income, commission income, or significant investment income, you can hire an accountant to assist you on income tax planning.

11. Create an investment policy

A good financial plan should have an investment policy statement that gives advice on how your portfolio should be invested.

When you write down your investment policy on paper, it will help you stay on track with investments when markets become volatile.

You can create a simple policy. For example, stating that you should invest in low cost, widely diversified ETFs or index funds that will be rebalanced annually to maintain 25% Canadian bonds, 25% US equities, 25% Canadian equities, and 25% international equities. The new money will be added to the lowest valued funds for you to buy low.

12. Create a will and keep it updated

Every adult with assets, children and a spouse should have a will. You need an accurate and up-to-date will so that your assets can be distributed the way you want after you have gone.

Financial planning doesn't end when you die. You should make provisions for what might happen to your property when you are gone. If you don't have a will, chances are the survivors will end up in court battling for your assets. Your assets might even end up disappearing.

Make some time and meet with a trusted attorney to come up with a will that distributes your assets according to your wishes.

Create one now and you can make adjustments in the future if your financial situation changes. All that's important is that actions are taken to prevent your assets from being the subject of conflict.

13. Save for retirement

Perhaps you've been saving for retirement, even if it's just a small amount every month. As soon as you get out of debt, your cash flow will increase, allowing you to save more money for retirement.

If you haven't started saving yet, start with an amount that won't hurt your financial situation. Your goal should be to increase your contribution every year.

You can achieve this by directing your future pay increase into the contribution. You can also increase it by redirecting debt payments once you've paid off debt. If you have a strong financial situation, you'll feel confident contributing a huge amount to your retirement plan, like bonus checks and income tax refunds.

14. Save for other goals

There are a lot of other reasons to save money. Saving for a future college education or a new car are perfect examples.

The reason to save for these other goals is so that more money is available for other expenses and so you can avoid getting into debt to pay for them.

It is no use to work hard to get out of debt, only to fall back into it when faced with a big expense.

Many people get stuck in a debt cycle they can never seem to recover from. That's why a good financial plan should include a prevention strategy. This involves saving money for things that will happen in the future.

You can set up an automatic weekly deposit into your savings account. You can save $150 per week instead of $500 per month. Smaller amounts may be more realistic than larger amounts.

15. Invest and diversify

When you have maxed out the eligibility on your retirement accounts, you can use other tools like annuities, mutual funds, or real estate to increase your investment portfolio.

You should diversify the types of investments you make. If you are careful and consistent with your investments, there will be a point where the investments make more money that you do. This is a great thing to have in place when you retire, especially since this is passive income.

When you are closer to retiring, you might want to change the way you invest. Make safer investments that won't be affected by market changes. This ensures that you have the money you need even if the economy crashes. When you are young, you have enough time for the market to recover. You can get a financial advisor if you need help with this.

Chapter 4 - Get out of debt

Many people have plans to pay off debt and most of them fail because they haven't identified their true motivation. You may start out fully motivated to repay all debt, but it's easy to become discouraged after making it past the initial stages.

If you want to keep your momentum, you need to continually remind yourself of the reasons you need to get out of debt. How will paying off your debt benefit you? What can't you do now that you can when you're debt-free?

If you haven't identified your true motivation, do so now. Your motivation is the reward you're striding towards. Defining it will make you realize just how much you want it, and how hard you're willing to work to achieve it.

Getting out of debt increases your financial security. It is a serious threat to financial security. The amount you spend on debt payments could have been saved for an emergency, retirement, or for your child's college fund. Being debt-free allows you to be financially secure.

Debt also prevents you from saving money for things you enjoy. Unfortunately, this is why people get deeper into debt. They can't afford the things they love so they make payments on credit until they can't borrow any more. Paying off all debt frees you from this vicious cycle and allows you to spend your income on what you enjoy.

Debt can also lead to more stress as you worry about covering debt payments as well as other expenses. A little stress occasionally isn't harmful, but stress all the time can lead to serious health issues like migraines and heart attacks. Becoming debt free can save your life.

What's unfortunate about debt is the more people you owe, the more bills you must keep up with. When you are debt free, you have fewer bills every month. You'll only have to worry about basic expenses like cell phone service, insurance, and utilities.

A debt-free person has a higher credit score. A huge debt, like credit card debt, will have a negative impact on your credit score.

A debt-free person also teaches their children good money habits by example. If you want your kids to stay away from debt, show them the importance of being debt-free and how to live a debt-free life.

Find out what causes debt

Have you ever considered the reason you're in a debt? Have you ever scrutinized these reasons? We all know that debt can lead us to disastrous consequences in our lives. Sometimes it consumes our assets, hurts our relationships, and brings about intense mental stress.

Many people have fallen deep into the black hole of financial debt. While we may know of the obvious reasons why, there are other factors that lead to debt accumulation.

Most people have spent their adult life in debt and there is nothing fun about it, but it doesn't have to define you.

Even though there are effective debt elimination programs like debt settlement and consolidation, we must be aware of the things that lead us to make great financial errors so that we can avoid them.

1. Failing to use money wisely

The first mistake that gets us into debt is overspending. Many people have gotten into financial trouble because they spent more than they could afford. This usually happens when you fail to set up a budget or create one and fail to stick to it.

Minimalist Budget

If you spend more than you earn, you must learn how to cut your expenses. And once you've cut your expenses, it's time to figure out how you can earn more money.

Another way that people fail to use their money wisely is by not getting insurance. This has made many individuals and businesses fall into huge debt. When you have an adequate insurance cover, especially health insurance, you will stay afloat during an emergency.

The same happens to small businesses. If a small business fails to take out general liability insurance or other insurance covers, they could face significant financial loss if an accident occurs or if they are sued. Business insurance is crucial to all businesses for basic protection.

Some people also fail to save for an emergency fund, so they get into huge debt when an emergency strikes. Even saving a small amount of money can make a big difference. Without an emergency fund, it can be hard to recover from an emergency. You'll have to use your savings or pay with credit. This can lead to a large accumulation of debt.

Some people get into a habit of gambling and end up losing a lot of money. Many view gambling as the best kind of entertainment, but it's just a guaranteed way of giving gambling companies your money. As loans are readily available these days, people are addicted to the idea of winning the lottery and becoming rich. Gambling can lead someone to throw their future away as they try to recover the money they have lost.

2. Life uncertainty

Sometimes things happen in our life that we don't expect and they end up causing financial problems. For instance, medical surgeries can be expensive. Medical costs and expenses can sometimes lead people into debt. If someone has gone through major medical surgery, chances are their insurance will not cover the full cost. Sometimes they may not be insured at all. When this happens, they could easily accumulate huge debt. It can be hard to avoid the massive cost of the procedure, but you can still find great hospitals that charge lower than the rest. You don't have to go to a specific hospital unless your insurance requires it.

Another uncertainty is inflation. Most people don't realize how much the cost of living has gone up. Between gas, food, and housing, and other expenses, most people won't receive a pay rise to offset these increases. If they can't cut back on spending, it might lead to more debt. If you leave your money in a regular savings account, your savings might be stripped due to inflation.

Another reason why people get into debt is a change of income. People will struggle to pay bills, and quickly suck up savings or turn to credit cards.

You might also move to a different house and the council tax band may become high. Perhaps your landlord increases your rent. The interest rate on a mortgage could also go up. How will you cope with these changes? This can easily send a person into debt.

Divorce can also present a strain on personal expenses. There are laws that govern what needs to be done with money during a divorce settlement. If one party demands too much, the other one might have to go into debt to pay for an attorney as well as what the other partner wants as part of the settlement.

4. Identity theft

Identity theft occurs when a criminal illegally opens up an account in your name and then runs up a huge amount of debt. The victim will be left with all the debt that someone else accumulated and they must pay for it. Identity theft cases have been on the rise and it could happen to anyone. To prevent such a disaster from happening to you, make sure that you keep all personal information as safe as possible. This includes your social security number and bank account numbers. Do not give this information to anyone unless you are 100% certain you can trust them. Bank officials usually have other ways of confirming your identity if they need to do so over the phone, so never be forthcoming with a caller who claims to be from your bank. In addition to these precautions, make sure to never leave important mail out in plain sight, where others can easily take hold of them.

5. Lack of financial knowledge

A lot of people don't have the financial experience or education required to make wise financial decisions. They may end up relying on credit cards or getting high-interest loans because they don't know what the best thing to do is. They may also fall for the tricks of many financial institutions. Often credit cards will be offered with seemingly fantastic benefits, and unbeknownst to the financially unaware target, the card will come with a myriad of hidden fees and high-interest. To avoid this, always go through the fine print and make sure you understand what it means.

Also, poor budgeting leads to debt. A person with good financial knowledge knows how important a monthly budget is. Without a good budget, you won't be able to track where your money goes. If you keep track of spending for a whole month, you will see exactly where your money goes and what you need to cut. This is where you can learn about unnecessary expenses. Without this, you can easily overspend and accumulate debt.

6. Expanding families

Many married and single people may feel they have a lot of extra money, but once they decide to have kids, that can change. Your expenses shoot up sharply with each child you have, sometimes more than people even expect. Sometimes families may have to forego one income, which can hurt their finances. If you don't have a kid, then you might not understand how day-care services can cost a lot, but it's something you should always keep in mind, if you're thinking of having a child. You'd be surprised by the amount of money that childcare costs. Make sure to consider all the expenses before you make this huge decision.

7. Taxes and high-interest charges

For most people, federal taxes have been flat for years, but state, produce, and local taxes have continued to increase. This means the average person has less spending money. There are taxes everywhere and the more money we make, the more we're taxed.

Many credit card accounts have interest rates that exceed 20%. This can make it impossible to repay debt. Many have fallen deep into debt because of credit cards.

8. Poor investments

People may have good intentions when they start investing but sometimes these investments turn out to be terrible choices and they end up losing money. This is why it's important to have a decent understanding on what you're investing in. Many people make the mistake of investing in things they barely comprehend.

Sometimes investing can be complicated, but it doesn't have to be. You need to be careful when investing or else you could incur major losses that are difficult to recover from. Consider keeping your investments simple or only making big choices when you have a complete understanding or the guidance of an expert.

9. Burying one's head in the sand

Failing to open emails on your doormat, avoiding phone calls from your creditors and ignoring financial issues will see you get into debt quickly.

Perhaps you don't have enough time to deal with your finances or you think that not opening your mail will make the situation go away. Both assumptions are completely wrong. When you fail to deal with the situation, things will just get worse and accumulate. If you are unable to pay a household bill, then call them. Explain to them why you can't pay and discuss plans. Stare that number in the face and come up with a plan for getting it settled.

Ignoring one bill might turn it into debt. Ignoring two bills might turn it into worse debt with added interest charges. You may even start seeing letters from a solicitor or a debt management company. They will start chasing these payments and this will affect your credit score. Fees will soon come as well. You may be taken to court and given a CCJ. Enforcement agents will turn up unannounced and knock on your door. To avoid this, pick up those calls and stop avoiding those letters.

10. Comparing yourself to others

Spending money because you think you need the same things as others will soon get you into debt. This is especially true if you cannot afford these things. Most people in society want something their neighbors have, but even if they acquire whatever it is they desire, they'll soon find that they hunger for something else. Desire can become a bottomless pit and unfortunately your money source is far from bottomless. Fashion changes every season and the media pushes products to manufacture desires. It doesn't matter what others are doing. Quit comparisons now. The liberation you'll feel will go beyond anything money can buy.

11 practical techniques to help you get out of debt - regardless of the amount

No matter what you are going through, whether you borrowed a loan or maxed out your credit card, it's your obligation to pay it back. Even if you've faced a life-changing experience like an accident, job loss, or an increase in expenses after having a child, debt will not suddenly decide to be kind.

Overspending can happen at any time of the year. Most people try to get out of debt, but life gets tougher and some end up giving up. This shouldn't be the case for you. There are a lot of people who get out of debt every day. Most people do it in a short amount of time.

If you've started a journey towards financial freedom, you should have a plan for how to handle debt. You may be wondering what the point is if you'll be financially free.

Think of that big project you're planning for. Perhaps it's a home renovation, a school or work assignment, or sorting the garage. Some projects are so daunting that we end up putting them off for a while.

A lot of people find it impossible to pay off debt because they deal with them in this manner.

They put off answering the phone, opening the mail, or making any kind of reparation because it seems too big a task. They act as if not looking at the problem will make it disappear.

As tempting as it can be to give into stagnation, the best way to tackle a huge project is to break up tasks into smaller achievable steps. This same rule applies to getting out of debt. Here are the techniques that will help you:

1. Pay off more than the minimum

If you have a credit card balance of about $15,000, and you pay a 15% APR, and make a minimum monthly payment of $600, it will take about 13 years to pay it off. That's only if you don't borrow more money in the meantime. This can be a huge challenge.

Whether you have a personal loan, credit card debt, or student loans, the best way to get out of debt soon is to pay more than the minimum monthly payment. When you do so, you'll save on interest while you repay the loan. It will help you pay off the debt sooner. To avoid headaches, ensure that your loan doesn't charge you prepayment penalties before getting started.

If you need help, there are many mobile and online repayment tools that will help you. They will help you track and chart your progress as you try to clear the balances.

2. Use excess cash to pay off debt

Whenever extra money fall into your lap, use it to speed up the debt repayment process. Some good examples of this unexpected money include an inheritance, profits from selling a car, a tax refund, and winnings from a bet. The more money you put towards debt repayment, the faster it will be cleared. Debt repayment doesn't have to take forever. Use the money you get from your annual raise or work bonus to speed things up.

Any time you get an unusual source of income, divert the money and use it wisely. You can even use the money to clear the smallest balance so that you can concentrate on the largest balance. Resist the tendency to see excess cash as money that you can spend on absolutely anything. As soon as you see excess money in your account, imagine how wonderful it will feel to deduct that excess amount from your debt instead. By paying off debt, you're indirectly making that surplus amount even higher! How? Cause paying off debt reduces your interest rate very slightly. You may regret buying another pair of shoes that looks exactly like another pair you own, but no one regrets paying off their debt.

3. Try the debt snowball method

Consider trying the debt snowball method to build momentum and speed up the debt repayment process.

The first step involves listing all your debts and arranging them from the smallest to largest. Whenever you have excess funds, start by repaying the smallest amount on the list. Consider making minimum payments on the larger loans. When the smallest balance has been paid off, start using the excess funds to repay the next smallest debt until you clear that one and so on.

As time goes by, you'll clear the smaller balances, and more money will be available to clear the larger loans. Clearing the smaller balances first means you'll see less loans on your list much sooner.

4. Get a part-time job

Eliminating debt with the snowball method might speed up the repayment process, but making more money can speed up the process even more.

Most people have a skill or a talent they can monetize. It could be babysitting, cleaning houses, mowing yards, or becoming a virtual assistant. If no talent comes to mind, check sites like Craigslist for one-time gigs that you can do on the weekends or evenings to make some extra cash.

Look for a part-time job in your area with a local retailer who might need seasonal workers to assist when the stores are busy. These part-time jobs can help you make enough money to get out of debt.

There are other seasonal jobs you can get. During springtime, there are a lot of farm and greenhouse jobs that can benefit you.

During the summer, you can try being a tour operator, landscaper or lifeguard. During the fall, there are seasonal jobs at pumpkin patches, haunted house attractions, and for fall harvest.

No matter the time of year, you will always find a temporary job to help with finances. All it takes is a little extra motivation and some creativity.

5. Make debt repayments as often as you can

This strategy pays off when it comes to taking care of your mortgage. When you make monthly payments, you will end up paying more interest and miss out on taking advantage of time.

Time will keep moving regardless of how you make your payments, so the easiest and least painful strategy to pay your mortgage loans is to accelerate payments

Change your monthly payment frequency to semi-monthly, weekly or bi-weekly. This will depend on how often you get a paycheck.

This change will save you money and time. The best strategy to tackle a big project is to break it into smaller steps.

Making frequent payments is also a perfect strategy to pay off your credit card debt. The more often you make payments, even if it's just with extra money, the less likely you are to waste it on something you won't need. If you want to get out of debt, find ways to make payments as often as you can.

6. Create and live with a bare-bones budget

If you want to get out of debt quickly, you should cut down on expenses as much as possible. You can use a bare-bones budget to help you with this. This strategy involves getting expenses as low as possible and living a simple life for as long as you can.

A bare-bones budget is different for everyone, but it should aim to eliminate all extra expenses like cable television, eating out, or other unnecessary spending.

You should remember that a bare-bones budget is meant to be used temporarily. When you are out of debt, or when you are closer to your goal, you can start adding these extras back into your budget.

Having a budget that tracks your income and expenses is important when it comes to getting out of debt in a short time. The budget will help you gauge your financial status so you can get closer to your goals.

A budget will show you whether you have surplus money, or if you have a deficit.

7. Try the laddering method

The laddering method involves listing all your debts, starting with debt that has the highest interest rate and ending with low-interest debt.

This method will save you a significant amount of time with continued use. You will be saving the money you would have used for interest when you clear debt with the highest interest. When you choose this strategy, you need to stick with it. Every month, put as much money as you can towards the debt with the highest interest rate, while still paying the required minimums on other cards. When the debt is paid off, divert the excess funds to the second debt with the second highest interest rate and so on. It is important not to close the account when you have paid off the balance. It will damage your credit. Just let the account sit without funds for a while.

If you have small debts that you can easily pay off, then do so. It will bring you tangible progress to get you started. When you have done that, start tackling the card with the highest interest rate.

8. Sell the things you don't need

If you are looking for a way to get some quick cash, consider selling some of your belongings. Most people have a lot of things in their homes that they don't need. These can range from outgrown clothes to finished books. Chances are there is a heap of stuff you've forgotten about that you'll likely never use again. Take a look around your home and rid yourself of the stuff that you forgot existed. Why not sell those items and use the money for something more worthwhile?

If you live in an area that permits an old-fashioned garage sale, then perhaps that will do. It is the easiest and cheapest way to unload unwanted belongings and make money. If that's not an option, consider selling them through an online reseller, consignment shop, or a Facebook yard sale group.

9. Avoid impulse spending

If saving extra money is what's holding you back, consider tracking your expenses for some weeks to know where your money goes. You might be surprised about your spending habits. Most people don't realize how quickly little expenses can add up. Perhaps you love grabbing a newspaper, buying coffee daily, getting takeout instead of making dinner. These can be categorized as impulse buys if they are purchases that seem to happen automatically. You are so sure you can afford this that you don't even think about it. Learn to make each buy intentional and resist the urge to buy impulsively. These spending habits will prevent you from saving enough money to clear your debt.

There are also other habits that cannot be noticed easily, for example, subscriptions to television channels that you never watch, downloading apps and ringtones, buying toys and gifts at a grocery store because it's convenient.

You can get almost everything you want any time at a local supercentre grocery store. If you want to get out of debt, make sure you avoid impulse purchases.

10. Ask for lower interest rates on credit cards and negotiate other bills

If credit card interest rates are high, it can be impossible to make headway on your balance. Consider calling your card issuer and negotiate. You may not know this, but asking for lower interest rates happens a lot. If you have a good history of paying your bills on time, chances are that you'll get a lower interest rate.

Other than credit cards, other bills can be negotiated down or eliminated. Remember the worst answer you can get is no. The less you pay for fixed expenses, the more money you get for debt payment.

If you are not the negotiating type, consider using apps that will review your purchase history. They'll find repeated fees and forgotten subscriptions you might want to cut from your budget.

11. Consider balance transfers

If a credit card company won't change their interest rates, perhaps it's a good idea to consider a balance transfer. There are a lot of balance transfer offers and you can secure a 0% APR for 15 months. However, you might have to pay a balance transfer fee of about 3% for the privilege.

Some cards don't charge a balance transfer fee for the first two months. They also offer a 0% introductory APR on purchases and balance transfers for the first 15 months.

If you have a credit card balance you can feasibly pay off during the time frame, transferring the balance to a card with 0% introductory APR could save you some money on interest while helping you pay down your debt faster.

It can be easy to continue living in debt if you have never faced the reality of the situation you are in. But when disaster hits, you'll gain a painfully new outlook quickly. One can also get sick of living a paycheck-to-paycheck lifestyle, and consider other ways to make ends meet.

No matter the type of debt you are in – whether it's from car loans, student loans, or another type of debt – it's crucial to know you can get out of it. It might not happen in a day, but a debt-free future can be achieved when one create a plan. You will have to stick to the plan for success.

No matter the plan you have, these strategies can help you get out of debt sooner than you thought. The faster you get out of debt, the quicker you can start living a life you've always wanted.

Chapter 5 - Make more with less

Whether you have some reserve in the tank or are living paycheck to paycheck, you're likely considering how to increase your income. How can you earn more money without losing more time in your day?

It's hard to persist when you have financial problems, but what other options do you have? At the end of the day, this comes down to how you use the money you have and your money mindset. There are a lot of benefits to positive thinking, but that alone isn't enough to help you increase your income.

You must act. That's what it takes. But before you act, you need to know what to do. How will you increase your income so you have enough money at the end of the month? First, you will have to learn how to maximize the use of your income, save enough money, and how to invest and build your personal assets.

Learn how to maximize the use of your income

If you find some extra money in your budget, chances are that you'll use it. While it might seem fun to use it on things you have always wanted, that's not a smart thing to do. The wisest thing to do is spend money on whatever can help you and your family.

You don't have to put all your money in a savings account. While it's good to save some money for difficult times, there are a lot of ways to maximize how you use your income. Although these purchases may not be fun to you, they can help you invest in your future. These wise ways to spend your money will help you live a happy life knowing you're using your money responsibly.

1. Pay off debt

If you want even more money to spend, pay off your debt. It is one of the smartest ways to spend your money. For instance, if you owe $2000 on a credit card and normally send the creditor $250 per month, why not use the tax return to pay off your debt? Then you'll have an extra $250 every month. While you may have plans for that money, clearing up $250 per month can make a huge difference in your budget.

2. Buy insurance

Insurance is one of those things we hope we never need, but if we have it when we need it, it can make a huge difference. You need to invest in a plan that will help you. For instance, having a health insurance plan helps to ensure that you always get affordable costs, should you get sick. This also applies to life insurance, home insurance, and auto insurance. When you have a good insurance plan, you are better equipped to handle life's unexpected events. When we put our income towards insurance, we make sure we have all we need in the future, should certain events occur.

3. Invest in a retirement plan

Another excellent way to maximize your income is by investing in a retirement plan. This will help you if you don't want to spend the rest of your life working. Consider investing in your future. If offered, consider having a 401(k) at work, and match what your employer contributes. If you want to take a step further, you can open an IRA. You will be required to invest each year, and the amount you pay will depend on your age.

4. Do home improvements

You don't want to buy a new window or roof until you must. However, investing in home improvements can increase your home's value. In some cases, these improvements can lower your electricity expenses. For instance, buying a new refrigerator can significantly reduce your electricity bill. Home improvements can increase the resale value of your home and turn it into an investment instead of a huge expense. Before doing home improvements, make sure to ask an expert what changes will raise the value of your home the most. Some improvements will be worth more than others.

5. Invest in education

It's always a good idea to invest your money in education. You can take a class to learn a new skill for a job, learn a new hobby, or start a new career or degree to help you get a promotion. A small price now could bring bigger earnings in, down the road.

Whatever your reasons are for investing in education, taking classes can be beneficial. Many will agree it's worth the time and money. In some instances, your employer might even reimburse you for the classes you take. Remember to check with your company first. You could also get tax benefits.

6. Attend a conference

Attending a conference is a great investment. You'll get the latest information about your area of expertise to help you be more successful at what you do. You can meet a lot of people and build a great network. If you are self-employed, it's a perfect way to let potential clients know about your services. You'll have access to a bigger pool of likely customers and this will increase your cash inflow.

Can you live on half your income and save the rest? Probably.

How soon could you achieve financial independence, if you could live on half of what you earn and invest the rest?

Probably within six years, and almost certainly less than ten years.

Minimalist Budget

You should note that retirement and financial independence are not just about how much you earn. It's about how much of your expenses you can pay off with the income from your investments.

You can speed up that process in two ways: increase investments and lower your expenses. Well, the good news is that these two goals can be achieved with the same process. It involves living on a percentage of your income and investing the rest to get more passive income.

Consider this challenge: assume that you can live on half your income and eliminate disbelief. What financial moves would you need to get there?

1. Make two-week's pay your new budget

When creating your monthly budget, you usually take four week's income into account. Occasionally you will get a bonus paycheck, but normally you'll receive paychecks for four weeks.

If you are normally paid biweekly, it means you receive two paychecks in a month. Your challenge would be how you can live on one pay

check. That's after taxes. That's your new budget.

Does it seem impossible? Well, what would happen if you lose your job tomorrow, spent the next six months without a job, and eventually got a job earning about half your income? Would you be out on the street? Would you starve?

No, you'd have to pay down your expenses and move on. That means its 100% possible to live on half your income. All you have to do is make some lifestyle changes.

Your new budget should only be one paycheck's worth of income. Start by writing your fixed monthly expenses. That includes fixed utility bills, car payment, housing, and other expenses. Then write down your variable expenses like gas for your car, usage-based bills, groceries, and others. And finally, write down semi-annual and annual recurring expenses, such as holiday gifts, insurance, accountant costs, etc.

When you have all that, just cut down unnecessary expenses to fit your new budget.

2. Eliminate or reduce housing costs

For most people, housing is the largest expense, and it's the first expense that you should scrutinize. Lucky for you, there is a way you can do this without moving to a less desirable home.

This involves getting a small multi-unit property, moving into one of the units, and leasing out the remaining units. The renters will contribute to the housing costs by paying you rent directly.

If you don't want to purchase a new home or move, there are still some options for you. You can segment part of your property as an income suite and then lease it out. You can sign a long-term lease agreement.

Or perhaps you can leave the whole separate income suite, and get a housemate. Housemates come with amazing advantages beyond paying rent. They help with house chores, cook meals, pay utility bills, and they can even become close friends.

If none of this sounds doable, then why not consider moving to a smaller home? A minimalist lifestyle will downsize your possessions so you may need less space than you did before. Perhaps even consider moving to a slightly less popular neighbourhood. All of these factors can reduce your rent significantly, and it doesn't necessarily mean your home is any less comfortable or attractive.

3. Learn to cook

Eating out or paying someone to cook for you can create huge expenses. They are budget killers and let's face it, they're not necessary.

Why don't you learn to cook? With time, you'll get better at it and you may even learn to enjoy it.

Anyone can learn to cook, and once you get over the initial awkwardness, you can learn to complete a three-course meal that beats anything at an overpriced restaurant. It will cost significantly lower prices to cook, and you can make extra food for the next day.

Also, when you cook for yourself, you'll end up cooking healthier meals than anything you'll find at a restaurant. You can pick low-carb or low-fat dishes and ingredients. Restaurants only prioritize taste, meaning excessive salt is often used.

4. Move your social life away from shopping

Where do you normally meet your friends? Bars? Movie theatres? Restaurants?

Since you can now cook, you can invite them over for dinner. You can also take cooler drinks somewhere with an amazing view instead of the bar. Instead of overpaying to get a movie ticket, plan a movie night at your or your friend's home. These days, movies can be rented online for a few dollars, and if you're tech savvy, they can even be streamed for free.

You could spend $100 eating out at a restaurant with friends, or you could spend $20 getting together for a bonfire or a picnic at the beach. Consider other options as well, such as a home wine-tasting or a backyard BBQ.

All it takes is a little more creativity and planning, but it will help you save an enormous amount of money without losing out on fun with friends.

5. Earn more money

If you are struggling to make ends meet with a two-week income, look for other ways to make more money. There are a lot of ways you can deal with this. You could negotiate for a pay rise at your workplace, or you could look for a new job that pays better. Find anything that can make you a more valuable employee and do it. If that's not possible, look for a part-time job to earn extra money.

What skills do you have that others need? Can you build websites on WordPress? Are you good at photography, and willing to work weddings for some weekend evenings every month? Do you have home improvement experience?

We all have skills, and everyone can learn to develop them. There are many ways to earn money, but it requires initiative on your part.

6. Automatically transfer half of your income

You will always be tempted to use money in your operating or checking account.

You can set up an automatic transfer from your account to an investment or savings account. You should do this transfer the same day you are paid.

In the beginning, you can use half of your income to pay off your debts. When all the debts are paid off, your budget will be very easy to deal with. With no debts, you can begin investing in high-yield investments that pay you. You will soon start rising, and you will be in a fantastic cycle where your income keeps on increasing.

That cycle will only take off if you keep expenses low. Most people only go out to spend when they get more money. They want a new car, fancy dinners out, a new house, and new clothes. That's what they call lifestyle inflation, and it's an enemy of financial independence.

7. Eliminate one money-draining habit

Alright, so maybe you're not ready to give up your entire lifestyle yet. In that case, start with one hobby or habit that costs you money every month. If you can't think of anything, check your most recent bank statement and highlight the deductions that went to wants, not needs. If you go to the movies a couple of times every month, stop going and stream your movies instead. If you enjoy purchasing stuff on Amazon every few weeks, stop doing it and replace it with a cheaper alternative like going to the library every few weeks. Once you've successfully eliminated a habit, you can continue you with your other money-wasting habits.

8. Push your mental boundaries

Our biggest limitations are our minds. Begin by working backward with your budget, cut your expenses down and boost your income. With discipline and creativity, it's possible to live on half your income. All it takes is your determination and perseverance.

Get the information you need to start investing

Do you want to invest but have no idea where to start? The first step to investing is the most important. If you invest wisely, it can lead to financial independence and passive income.

If you want to start investing, you need to have the right information so you avoid wasting your money on poor investments. So, what information should you have to get started? Here is what you need to know to ensure your investment is a success:

1. **Decide on the type of assets you want to own**

Investing is about putting money in something today and getting more money out of it in the future. Usually, you can achieve that by acquiring productive assets. For instance, if you buy an apartment building, you will own the property and the cash that it produces through rent.

Each productive asset has unique characteristics as well as pros and cons. Here are some of the potential investments you might consider:

Business equity – Owning equity in a business enables you to share a profit or loss generated by the company. Whether you want to own that equity by buying shares of a publicly traded business or acquiring a small business outright, business equities are the most rewarding asset class.

Fixed income securities - When you decide to invest in fixed income security, you are lending money to a bond issuer. In exchange, you will get an interest income. You can do so in many ways: from US saving bonds to tax-free municipal bonds, from corporate bonds to money markets and certificates of deposit.

Real estate – Real estate is perhaps the most easily understood and oldest asset class investors. You can make money by investing in real estate in several ways, but it comes down to either owning something and letting others use it for lease payments or rent, or developing property and selling it for profit.

Intangible property and rights – Intangible property consist of everything from patents and trademarks to copyrights and music royalties.

Farmland and other commodity-producing goods – investment in commodity-producing activities involve extracting or producing something from nature or the ground. It usually involves improving it and selling it to make a profit. If there is oil on your land, you can extract it and get cash. If you grow corn, you can sell it and make money. It can involve a lot of risks – disasters, weather, and other challenges that might make you lose money – but you can still make money from it.

2. Decide how you want to own these assets

When you have decided on the assets you want to own, you can decide how you to own them. To understand this point, let's look at business equity. Let's say you want a stake in a publicly traded business. Will you go for shares outright or will you go through a pooled structure?

- **Outright ownership** – This way, you will directly buy shares from an individual company and you will see them in your balance sheet or that of the entity you own. You will be an actual share shareholder and have voting rights. It might give you access to dividend income. Your net worth might rise as the company grows.

- **Pooled ownership** – With this method, you will add your money to a pool contributed to by other people and buy ownership through a shared entity or structure. Most of the time, this is done through mutual funds. If you are a wealthy investor, you can invest in hedge funds. If you don't have a large amount of money, you can consider investing index funds and exchange-traded funds.

3. Decide where you want to hold the assets

When you have made up your mind on how you want to acquire investment assets, you need to decide how you want to hold these assets. There are several options:

- **Taxable account** – If you decide on taxable accounts like a brokerage account, you will pay tax later but there won't be any restrictions on your money. You will be free to spend it on anything you want. You will be free to cash in and buy anything you want. You can also add any amount you want to it every year.

• **Tax shelters** - If you choose to invest in things like Roth IRA or 401(k) plan, there are tax and asset protection benefits. Some retirement plans and accounts offer unlimited bankruptcy protection. This means that should a medical disaster strike that wipes out your balance sheet, the creditors won't touch your investment capital. Some are tax-deferred. This means you might get tax deductions when you deposit the capital into an account to choose investment and pay taxes in the future. Good tax planning can mean massive extra wealth in the future.

• **Trust other asset protection mechanisms** – You can hold your investments through structures or entities like trust funds. You will get major asset protection and planning benefits when you use these special ownership methods. This is useful when you want to restrict how your capital is used. Also, if you have significant real estate investments or operating assets, you can speak to your attorney to set up a holding company.

The information you need to start building your personal assets

There are a lot of ways to build personal assets with little money, but few people know how to do it. What could be the problem? The problem is most people don't know about the important process of asset building.

What should one do to build assets? It's not rocket science. If you learn the process of asset building, the rest is easy.

Invest money to accumulate assets

You should know all about the relationship between asset accumulation and investments.

- **Investments** – Investing is the process of buying assets. Investments are generally made in either stocks, bonds, or cash equivalents. Investments are made with the intention of generating income and earning profits over time. When investments succeed, they are a great way to make passive income. In other words, money gets made without the need for daily upkeep.

- **Asset accumulation** – When you gradually acquire assets over time and hold it for the long term, assets will start to accumulate. These assets consist of your earnings, savings, and the returns on your investments.

- **Asset building** – Asset building is the process of gradually buying assets or acquiring resources with the intention of accumulation. This practice can help families achieve stability, create good credit, save for the future, and ultimately strengthen their communities.

When you buy assets without the intention of accumulation, it becomes a meaningless activity. Without them, it is much more difficult to save for the future.

Since you now understand the process of asset building, let's ask a more basic question.

Why build assets?

If you're interested in achieving financial independence, then you'll want to consider building assets. Why is that necessary?

Do you love your job? I know few people who would raise their hands to that question. If most people don't love their jobs, why do they keep them? It's simple: we need the money so we feel we don't have another choice. It all comes down to the basic need for survival. We think our jobs are inextricably linked to this.

We must compromise to do our jobs because we want to continue earning income. Is there a way to remove this dependency? You may not believe this, but it's absolutely possible. All you have to do is make the necessary changes to your lifestyle and spending habits to achieve financial independence. It's much easier than you think. Here is an approach to help you.

• Realize that you depend on your job for income and understand that there is an alternative. Most people who work don't realize that financial independence exists.

• Start eliminating financial dependence gradually. You can do this by generating an alternative source of income. Where will your alternative source of income come from? From investing in assets. Consider which assets will add the biggest value to your life.

How can a common man build assets?

For those who are already affluent, asset building methods are different. How can a common man build assets? Here are the steps:

1. Save – Saving money is very important. The easiest way one can save money is by putting aside some of their income. Eliminating unnecessary spending will increase cash-in-hand. Even millionaires must save money if they want to stay rich. If you save above 25% of your total income, that is considered a decent saving. You can make an automatic transfer where 25% of your money goes automatically to your savings account.

Saving money also allows you to have more money to invest with. When you make larger investments, you can expect bigger returns when the money multiplies.

Here are some other ideas to help you keep more money in your bank account.

- **Build an emergency fund** – Nothing eats assets faster than an emergency. When something unexpected happens, it can consume a lot of money. An example is a medical emergency. It's recommended that you keep sufficient back-up to handle emergencies. Consider saving for an emergency in cash and insurance.

- **Arrange a recurring deposit** – The priority here is to save. You shouldn't think about a return. There are some advantages to recurring deposits. Savings will be automatic, money is safe, and money remains in the bank.

    Building an emergency fund ensures that we are prepared to meet life's emergencies. When they happen, we can depend on our savings. Arranging for recurring deposits ensures that what we save can be used for investments.

2. **Invest** – Why do you need to invest and not keep building savings to buy assets directly? It would be nice to do that, but holding your money as savings isn't recommended. That's because savings can easily be spent. And don't forget, investing your money makes it multiply.

When you have gone through all the effort of saving, you should ensure that you invest that money wisely. Most people have no idea how. Here are some examples of different investments you can make. Many investment experts even advise utilizing more than one method.

- **Hybrid funds** – Hybrid funds have a SIP, which is a useful tool for investments. There are several benefits. You will get exposure to debt and equity from one window. You should develop a mindset to keep you investing in this fund through SIPs. Keep doing this month after month without stopping.

- **Index ETFs** – ETFs, also known as Exchange-Traded

Funds, can make a worthwhile investment and can encompass many types of investments, such as bonds, stocks, and other types.

ETFs offers great investment diversification within an equity portfolio. You can get ETF units every time there is above a 3% dip in an index.

- **Gold** – Gold can be a long-term investment that takes up to 12 years. Unlike the other forms of investments, you can actually hold this investment in your own hands.
- **Buy land** – Land is an asset that has become scarce. It's a great idea to invest in land on the outskirts of a city, though all investments in land can be risky. This is because it doesn't produce an income unless you do something with it, and in the meantime, it can cost you a lot in taxes. If you're considering investing in land, make sure you have a plan, and it may be wise to talk to an expert.
- **Trade Cryptocurrencies** – This method of investing is not devoid of its risks, but many people insist there's a lot more money to be made in cryptocurrency investments. In recent years, many bitcoin investors have made fortunes, though many have also lost. Cryptocurrencies can bring you big rewards when invested in wisely. We advise educating yourself before purchasing any.

3. **Locked funds** – This step is very important. Most people would stop at step two. In this step, you will be converting all your assets

into income generating assets. How can this be done? You can consider REITs, rental properties, and dividend-paying stocks.

Since the above steps are very crucial to asset building, let's go into more detail on how we can implement them successfully.

The money you locked in land, SIP, and RD has only one objective. You can redeem it and use it to buy assets at some point. You can use it on income generating assets. Consider the following:

- **Dividend-paying stocks** – These are strong stocks which pay regular dividends to the shareholder. You should buy these stocks at the right price. If you fail to do so, its yield will be too low. You should wait for a perfect time to get the best dividend paying stocks.
- **Rental property** – This might be the best income generating asset you can get, as it generates the best passive income and depending on the property, this passive income can be a sizable sum. What you earn from real estate property also increases the rate of inflation.

You should consider distributing your investments among the above options. These are perfect investment vehicles for income generation.

What's the difference between trading and investing?

Both trading and investing involve making a profit by buying and selling stocks. What sets them apart, however, is how they go about achieving those goals. Trading is more concerned with using the stock market for short-term gains, while investments are usually a long-term commitment that takes place over years and sometimes even decades.

Trading involves higher risks than investing, but also higher returns. This is because stock prices can fluctuate a lot within a short period of time. Timing is, in fact, a major factor that needs to be considered, in the world of trading.

Investing is significantly lower in risk, but don't expect any big returns right away. Investments can get you big rewards, but these will take some time.

How to make successful investments and get big rewards

Now that you're no longer relying on material goods, you likely have more money to spare for your investments. You may even be interested in stocks. Although it may seem simple at first glance, there's a lot more to trading and investing than simply making a purchase and waiting for the dough to roll in. For the most fruitful outcome, you must stay informed on a variety of different factors.

When it comes to buying stocks, it's not enough to just make any investment or trade. In fact, investing in the wrong thing could result in a major loss. To win big from an investment, you need to make calculated efforts in the right direction. You must consider all your options carefully and resist the urge to throw your money at absolutely anything. To ensure that both your trades and investments are successful, keep these useful tips in mind.

1. Don't just fall for the idea

Let's face it, in this day and age, everyone has a good idea. And as for the great ideas out there, chances are that someone has had the same one before. For this reason, you shouldn't throw your money at just any good idea. Take other factors into account. Which company is in charge of this good idea? What is their business plan? There are many reasons why a good idea could lead to a loss or nothing at all. Instead of falling for the idea, fall for the company instead.

2. Always do the research

You may get a good feeling right from the get-go, but good feelings can be wrong. Don't let your financial future suffer for it. Traders should always do their research. Not just into various companies, but also trading patterns and other trends. Resist the urge to wing it and stay completely informed on the entire trading landscape. Understand that everything can affect what happens to your hard-earned money.

3. Spread out your investments

A good tip for avoiding huge losses is to make sure you don't invest in solely one company. Instead, try spreading out your investments between a few different options. Learn from the old saying, "Don't keep all your eggs in one basket." It rings particularly true for investing. This way, if any loss occurs, it won't be catastrophic and you'll still have stocks in other companies. If disaster strikes a company you've invested in, you won't make a huge loss. It may seem unlikely for this to happen, but this is exactly the type of attitude that can lead to losses from carelessness. Many investors have lost billions by failing to take this precaution. For example, in the Enron company scandal.

4. Take some risks

Studies have shown that the crushing disappointment we feel when we lose money is greater than the joy we feel when we win. To avoid these negative feelings, many investors and traders avoid making any risks at all in their pursuits. While we don't advise making big risks all the time, it can pay off to take a leap every now and then. Sometimes you can get very lucky. Just make sure that, should a loss occur, it won't affect your financial standing in a significant way. Make smart risks and you just might find yourself making big returns.

5. Don't overestimate your abilities

After all the time and effort spent staring at the screen, you've finally made a return. Congrats! While this is definitely something to celebrate, don't let your winners' high cloud your judgment. You're not invincible and you could easily lose it all if you don't continue to be careful. Rewards don't always indicate the skill of a trader, sometimes it can all be down to luck. Don't take any wild risks on an impulse. Always invest wisely.

Remember to try and enjoy the world of investing. While it's true that there are many risky aspects to it, it'll bring you more satisfaction and control than putting that same money in needless items. To truly honor the minimalist philosophy, only invest in what you really believe in, and resist the urge to invest in everything.

Greater life satisfaction will come when you take control of your finances back from every whim, fleeting desire and impulse. This is the minimalist way.

Conclusion

Thank you for making it to the end of the Minimalist Budget Mindset.

Let's hope it was informative and able to provide you with all the information you need to manage your money well and achieve your financial goals. With more tools in your money-saving arsenal, you'll find it much easier to take those strides towards financial freedom.

You have learned that minimalism can put an end to the gluttony of the world that surrounds us. It's the opposite of what you see in advertisements on TV. We live in a society that prides itself on buying a lot of needless products; we are overwhelmed by consumerist habits, clutter, material possessions, debt, noise, and distractions. What we don't seem to have enough of, however, is true meaning in our lives and intentionality in our actions. With all you've learned, you'll find it much easier to shut out the noisy consumerist world, with its many money-grabbing ploys.

Adopting a minimalist lifestyle will allow you to eliminate the things you don't need so you can concentrate on what really completes your life. Once you start shifting your values, the money-saving techniques we've demonstrated we'll feel like second nature.

You have learned exactly how you can save money as a minimalist. Saving money this way has a lot of benefits and it could save you a lot of distress in the future. You have learned how to track your spending and how you can start saving money. This has taught you how to be disciplined when money is involved.

Other than that, you have learned some of the best budgeting strategies to help you achieve your goals. Apply these strategies as soon as you can to achieve financial goals sooner than you expect. Don't feel daunted, as you may find them easier than you think.

Getting out of debt has never been easy for most of us, but learning about the causes of debt has helped you view debt differently and learn effective ways to get out of it. These methods will help you get out of debt while at the same time helping you save more.

When you have eliminated debt and learned how to save, consider investing in something that will multiply your money. With the information you have learned about investing, and the life-altering self-discipline you have gained, you will view investing from a different angle and start accumulating personal wealth. Use your newly discovered tips wisely to ensure you minimize any potential losses and make more frequent gains.

You've now learned how to develop a minimalist mindset and make the big savings that all successful minimalists do. Practice makes perfect, and that's what you need to do with your new minimalist budget mindset. With some time and practice, you will be able to make use of good money habits and make it your part of life.

Lastly, if you enjoyed this book I ask that you please take the time to review it on Audible.com. Your honest feedback would be greatly appreciated.

Thank you.

www.ingramcontent.com/pod-product-compliance
Lightning Source LLC
Chambersburg PA
CBHW031109080526
44587CB00011B/894